The Joy of Apples

by Theresa Millang

Adventure Publications, Inc.
Cambridge, Minnesota

A special thank you to all.

A special thank you to my friends and other contributors to this collection. Apples are enjoyed fresh and also cooked in both sweet and savory recipes. I have included all my favorite recipes, and also the recipes I have collected from across the country. So, a salute to apples, and to all who added to this collection.

Book and Cover Design by Jonathan Norberg

Copyright 2005 by Theresa Nell Millang
Published by Adventure Publications, Inc.
820 Cleveland Street South
Cambridge, Minnesota 55008
1-800-678-7006
www.adventurepublications.net

ISBN-13: 978-1-59193-123-2
ISBN-10: 1-59193-123-1
Printed in China

Table of Contents

A BIT OF APPLE HISTORY 13

GROWING FACTS 13

SELECTION AND STORAGE 14

HEALTH BENEFITS OF APPLES 15

APPLE FUN FACTS 16

WEIGHTS AND MEASURES 16

COBBLERS, CRUNCHES, CRISPS
Cobblers
Apple Cobbler 18
Apple-Cranberry Cobbler 19
Apple Dumpling Cobbler 20
Cake Mix Apple Cobbler 21
Gingerbread Apple Cobbler 22

Crumbles
Cake Mix Apple Crumble 23
Granny Smith Apple Crumble 24
Rhubarb-Apple Crumble 25

Crisps
Apple Crisp 26
Apple-Cherry Crisp 27
Cranberry-Apple Crisp 28
Mary Dow's Applesauce Crisp 29
Microwave Apple Crisp 30

CAKES, COFFEECAKES, CHEESECAKES

Cakes

Apple Upside-Down Cake 32
Autumn Surprise Cake 33
Cake Mix Applesauce Bundt Cake 34
Caramel Apple Pudding Cake 35
Caramel-Glazed Apple Pound Cake 36
Caramel-Topped Apple Cake 37
Cream Cheese-Frosted Apple Cake 38
Fudge Nut Applesauce Cake 39
Lemon-Apple Cake 40
Minnesota Apple Pudding Cake 41
Sandra's Fresh Apple Cake 42
Sauerkraut Apple Cake 43
Spicy Apple Cake 44
Streusel Apple Loaf Cake 45

Coffeecakes

Apple Cream Cheese Coffeecake 46
Apple Walnut Coffeecake 47
Pecan Streusel Coffeecake 48

Cheesecakes

Apple Cheesecake 49
Baked Apple Cheesecake 50

BARS, SQUARES, COOKIES

Bars

Apple Cheesecake Bars 52
Coconut Apple Bars 53
Frosted Apple Bars 54

Granny Smith Apple Caramel Bars 55
Lemon-Glazed Apple Brownie 56
Lola's Applesauce Bars 57
Minnesota Cream Cheese-Frosted Apple-Cranberry Bars 58
Zucchini Applesauce Bars 59

Squares
Butterscotch Apple Squares 60
Caramel Apple Oat Squares 61
Saucy Caramel Apple Squares 62
Sour Cream Apple Squares 63
Streusel Apple Squares 64

Cookies
Glazed Apple Cookies 65
Kiki's Applesauce Cookies 66
Peanut Butter Applesauce Cookies 67
Sesame Apple Cookies 68

PIES
Apple Almond Pie 70
Apple-Blueberry Cheddar Crumb Pie 71
Apple Butter Pie 72
Apple Buttermilk Custard Pie 73
Apple Chess Pie 74
Apple-Cranberry Pie 75
Apple Cream Pie 76
Apple Pecan Upside-Down Pie 77
Applesauce Pie 78
Baked Little Apple Pies 79
Caramel Apple Crumb Pie 80

Cranberry-Apple Streusel Custard Pie 81
Deep Dish Apple Pie. 82
Double Crusted Apple Pie 83
Fried Apple Pies 84
Glazed Apple-Rhubarb Pie. 85
Impossible French Apple Pie 86
No-Bake Apple Pie. 87
Pumpkin-Apple Pie. 88
The Big Apple Apple Pie 89
Zucchini-Apple Cream Pie. 90

DESSERTS

Apple Brown Betty 92
Apple Charlotte 93
Apple Cheddar Quesadillas 94
Apple Crème Brûlée 95
Apple Custard Enchiladas 96
Apple Dumplings 97
Apple Flan 98
Apple Kuchen. 99
Apple Lasagna 100
Apple Pandowdy. 101
Apple Sorbet 102
Apple Strudel 103
Baked Apples. 104
Caramel Apple Dessert 105
Caramel Apple Shortcakes 106
Cheddar-Stuffed Baked Apples 107
Creamy Apple Ricotta Bread Pudding. 108
Micro-Baked Apples 109
Pecan Apple Dumplings with Sauce. 110

Steamed Apple Pudding 111
Walnut Apple Cream Cheese Dessert 112

TARTS, TORTES

Tarts

Apple-Cranberry Pecan Tart. 114
Apple Tart 115
Apple Tarte Tatin. 116
Minnesota Apple Cream Cheese Tart 117

Tortes

Apple Torte. 118
Bavarian Apple Torte. 119
Applesauce Torte 120
Golden Delicious Apple Torte. 121
Linzer Apple Torte. 122

MUFFINS, BREADS

Muffins

Apple-Carrot Muffins. 124
Apple Cheddar Muffins 125
Apple-Cranberry Muffins 126
Apple Streusel Muffins 127
Applesauce Bran Muffins. 128
Rhubarb Applesauce Muffins 129
Sam's Apple Muffins. 130

Breads

Apple Butter Bread. 131
Apple Corn Bread 132
Apple Quick Bread 133

Apple Strudel Machine Bread 134
Apple Whole Wheat Bread 135
Applesauce Raisin Bread. 136
Chocolate Applesauce Bread. 137
Fresh Lemon Poppyseed Applesauce Loaf. 138

SCONES, BISCUITS, POPOVERS, FRITTERS, DOUGHNUTS, TURNOVERS

Scones

Apple Cheddar Scones 140
Apple-Cranberry Scones 141

Biscuits

Applesauce Biscuits 142

Popovers

Apple Popovers 143

Fritters

Apple Fritters 144

Doughnuts

Applesauce Doughnuts 145

Turnovers

Cheese Apple Turnovers 146

APPETIZERS

Baked Applesauce Sausage Appetizer 148
Cranberry-Apple Baked Brie 149
Mr. Brown's Country Ribs 150

SALADS, SOUPS

Gelatin Salads

Applesauce Raspberry Gelatin Salad 152
Cherry-Apple Cream Cheese Gelatin Mold 153
Cranberry Applesauce Gelatin Salad. 154

Other Salads

Avocado-Apple Chicken Salad 155
California Apple-Veggie Salad 156
Chicken Waldorf Salad 157
Chicken Apple Salad. 158
Grilled Chicken Apple Salad. 159
Waldorf Turkey Salad 160
Apple-Cranberry Salad with Sour Cream Dressing. 161
Apple Poppyseed Slaw 162
Apple-Spinach Salad. 163
Apple Salad with Boiled Dressing. 164
Cran-Apple Salad 165
Date-Apple-Pineapple Salad 166
Louisiana Sweet Potato Apple Salad 167
Orange-Cranberry-Apple Salad 168
Spinach-Apple Salad. 169
Waldorf Apple Salad 170
Wisconsin Caramel Apple-Cranberry Salad 171

Soups

Apple Barley Soup 172
Carrot-Apple Soup 173
Curried Apple-Cauliflower Soup 174
Gouda Cheese Apple Soup 175
Yam-Apple Soup. 176

MEALS PAIRED WITH APPLES

Apple Cheese Strata. 178
Apple Cinnamon Quesadillas 179
Apple Sage Breakfast Sausage 180
Apple Pecan Oven Pancake 181
Applesauce Waffles 182
Brie Apple Omelet 183
Gruyere Apple Frittata. 184
Oven Apple French Toast 185
Sour Cream Apple Pancakes. 186
Apple Butter Grilled Pork Country Ribs 187
Apple Chicken Stir-Fry 188
Apple Ham Cheddar Sourdough Sandwiches 189
Apple Pork Curry 190
Beef and Apple Stir-Fry. 191
Brie Apple Baked Chicken Breasts 192
Chicken Tacos with Apples 193
Honey Mustard Pork Roast with Apple Stuffing. 194
Pork Apple Wraps. 195
Pork Tenderloin with Apples. 196
Slow Cooker Apple Pork Tenderloins 197
Turkey Breast with Sausage Apple Stuffing 198

STUFFING, SIDES

Stuffing

Almond Brown Rice Apple Stuffing 200
Apple Pecan Baked Stuffing 201
Cranberry-Apple Stuffing. 202
Fresh Apple-Cranberry Corn Bread Stuffing 203
Herb Apple and Sausage Corn Bread Stuffing 204
Sausage Apple Chestnut Stuffing 205

Sides

Acorn Squash with Apple Stuffing 206
Apple Cider Baked Beans 207
Apple Rings and Yams 208
Brussels Sprouts with Apples 209
Carrot-Apple Bake 210
Moose's Apple-Sweet Potato-Pineapple Bake 211
Red Cabbage with Apples 212
Ruth's Whipped Apple-Sweet Potato Bake 213
Scalloped Apples with Cranberries 214
Spiced Apples 215
Sweet Potatoes with Chunky Applesauce 216

BEVERAGES

Citrus Cider Punch 218
Hot Buttered Cider 219
Hot Cider Wassail 220
Spiced Apple Tea 221
Apple-Raspberry Punch 222

SAUCES, CONDIMENTS

Sauces

Apple Cider Barbecue Sauce 224
Applesauce 225
Apple-Cranberry Sauce 226
Microwave Three-Apple Applesauce 227

Condiments

Apple Chutney 228
Apple Jalapeño Salsa 229
No-Cook Cranberry-Apple-Orange Relish 230

Apple Syrup 231
Nelan's Apple-Flavored Syrup 232

JAMS, JELLIES, PRESERVES, APPLE BUTTER
Pear-Apple Jam 234
Apple Jelly 235
Apple Preserves 236
Apple Butter 237
Crockpot Apple Butter 238

MISCELLANEOUS
Aplets 240
Apple Chips 241
Apple Peanut Butter Dip 242
Apple Nut Granola 243
Chocolate Peanut Butter Fondue with Apple Dippers 244
Favorite Caramel Apples 245
Turtle Caramel Apples 246

CRAB APPLES
Crab Apple Butter 248
Crab Apple Jam 249
Crab Apple Jelly 250
Crab Apple Hot Pepper Jelly 251
Crab Apple Quick Bread 252
Green Apple-Crab Apple Pie 253
Spiced Crab Apples 254

ABOUT THE AUTHOR 255

A Bit of Apple History

Apples have had a place in stories throughout history, from Greek tales of the Golden Apples to Snow White. Historical figures associated with apples include the Swiss hero William Tell, Sir Isaac Newton and, of course, Johnny Appleseed. While not all historians agree as to the location where apples were first cultivated, most credit the Romans with major advances in pomology (the study and cultivation of fruit) and the widespread introduction of cultivated apples across their vast empire.

Though there are native North American varieties of wild apples, most of the "wild" apples that are found today were introduced during colonial times and later escaped cultivation. Colonists brought seeds and saplings from their homes to start their own orchards in the New World. One man, John Chapman, later nicknamed Johnny Appleseed, owned parcels of land across Illinois, Ohio and Indiana. Around 1800, he moved from his home in Massachusetts and began an early nursery service. He planted apple seeds on his tracts of land and sold seeds and saplings to settlers moving west. In this way, he was responsible for helping cultivated apples spread across the nation. The first apples from America were exported around 1768.

Today there are approximately 7,500 varieties of cultivated apples. About 2,500 of these are grown in the U.S. Major apple-producing states are Washington, New York, California, Pennsylvania, Virginia and Michigan, though apples are grown in all 50 states. In the U.S., only oranges are of higher commercial value than apples. On average, each person in America eats about 65 fresh apples per year—that's almost 20 pounds.

Growing Facts

Apples are a member of the rose family, which also includes pears and cherries. Apple trees benefit from good air flow and grow best in rich, well-drained soils. Apple blossoms are situated in clusters, with a large central "king" blossom and a few smaller blossoms around it. The king will set the largest fruit. Many apple growers keep beehives in their orchards during blossom time to promote pollination.

Trees are pruned and trained to develop strong, healthy structures that will support full loads of ripe apples.

If you'd like to plant your own backyard orchard, start with just a pair of trees. You'll need two trees for good pollination. Consider dwarf varieties (you won't need a ladder to pick your harvest!) with good disease resistance. Local orchards and nurseries can be of great help; it's worth checking with them for suggestions and tips for success.

Selection and Storage

Part of the reason why apples are so popular is that there are thousands of varieties. Some are better for sauces or cider, and some are best enjoyed raw. A good way to learn about different apples is to visit a local apple orchard. Most orchards will provide information and special uses for the varieties of apples they grow. You're sure to find a few new favorites!

Apples like to be kept cool (close to 40° F) and they like higher humidity than most other fruits. Depending on the storage conditions and apple variety, apples can keep from harvest until the following spring. If you're storing apples long-term, check them periodically to make sure that none are spoiled or shriveled. Apples stored at room temperature ripen and lose their quality ten times faster than refrigerated apples.

Freezing Apples Without Sugar
Apples frozen without sugar are suitable for cooking and pie making. Wash, peel, core and slice apples. To prevent darkening, dissolve ½ teaspoon (1500 mg) ascorbic acid powder or equivalent of crushed vitamin C tablets in 3 tablespoons water. Sprinkle over apples. Browning can also be prevented by dipping apple slices in orange or pineapple juice, or in a mixture of ¼ cup lemon juice to 1 quart of water. Place apple slices in zip-closure freezer bags, label, date and freeze. Treated apples can also be frozen first on a tray, leaving space between each piece. Pack into containers as soon as slices are frozen (about 2–4 hours). Freeze up to one year at 0° F or below.

Sun Drying Apples

Pick firm apples for drying. Wash, core and peel the apples, then slice into rings or ¼-inch thick wedges. Dip apple slices in an ascorbic acid mixture (¼ cup lemon juice to 1 quart water) to keep them from turning brown as they dry. Lay treated slices on trays and cover with cheesecloth. Place the trays in a well-ventilated area full sunlight. Turn slices every few hours.

Health Benefits of Apples

Apples are a great package. There's no need to peel them—in fact, the lion's share of the nutrients in apples are in the skin—and you don't need to pick many to fill your basket. Apples keep much longer than other fruits, and can be used in a huge variety of dishes. Plus, they have incredible health benefits.

One medium-sized unpeeled apple contains only 80 calories and is considered to be fat-, sodium- and cholesterol-free. You'll also get vitamin C, calcium, potassium, phosphorous and boron, which is good for keeping bones strong. Apples contain good amounts of pectin, a soluble fiber that can help prevent buildup of cholesterol in blood vessels, as well as insoluble fiber, which supports a healthy intestinal tract. A medium apple contains about 5 grams of fiber: the equivalent to a bowl of bran cereal. The fiber in apples is also a good tool for weight loss by providing bulk for digestion without lots of calories. The fiber in apples has another important function. Because of all the fiber present in apples, the sugar (mostly fructose) is released slowly into the bloodstream, preventing spikes in blood-sugar levels.

Phytonutrients, a group of nutrients found in apples and other fruits and vegetables, are plant chemicals that have antioxidant power. Antioxidants stabilize free radicals, which are thought to cause or accelerate many health problems, mostly associated with aging. Our bodies produce free radicals through normal metabolic processes, but we also accumulate free radicals from our environment. Toxic levels of free radicals have been blamed for the cell damage that causes cancer, heart disease and age-related disorders such as Alzheimer's. A diet that includes antioxidant-rich apples can help ward off this kind of cell damage.

The nutrients in apples and apple juice can help protect against cancers such as stomach, prostate, lung and breast cancer, and also associated tumor growth. Apple nutrients can also help prevent and ease symptoms of chronic respiratory illnesses, which include asthma. In addition, apples can help to lower "bad cholesterol" (LDL) and protect heart and artery health. Some studies show that apples can reduce the risk of type 2 diabetes. Apples are good for the brain, too. Studies at the University of Massachusetts-Lowell suggest that apples and apple juice can improve memory and learning and help maintain the brain's performance.

So pick an apple and enjoy all the health benefits of this crisp treat!

Apple Fun Facts

Apples float because their volume is approximately 25% air.
Some apple trees can produce for more than 100 years.
The largest apple on record weighed just over 3 pounds.

Weights and Measures

1 pound equals:
3 medium apples
2 cups sliced
1½ cups applesauce

3 pounds equals:
8–9 medium apples
one 9" pie

1 peck equals:
10–12 pounds
32 medium apples
3–4 9" pies

1 bushel equals:
42–48 pounds
126 medium apples
15 9" pies
about 18 quarts of applesauce

Sources: www.bestapples.com/healthy/ (Accessed 05/27/05); www.urbanext.uiuc.edu/apples/ (Accessed 05/27/05); www.nutritionj.com/content/3/1/5 (Accessed 05/27/05); www.pepinheights.com/an_apple_a_day/apples_FAQs.php (Accessed 05/27/05); www.usapple.org/consumers/dailyapple/index.shtml (Accessed 05/27/05); www.usapple.org/media/newsreleases/index.shtml (Accessed 05/27/05)

Cobblers
Crumbles
Crisps

APPLE COBBLER

Serve warm with vanilla ice cream.

8 large, tart cooking apples, peeled, cored and sliced ¼-inch thick
¾ cup granulated sugar
½ teaspoon ground cinnamon

2 cups all-purpose flour
2 cups granulated sugar
¼ teaspoon ground cinnamon
2 teaspoons baking powder
¾ teaspoon salt
2 eggs
1 teaspoon pure vanilla extract
½ cup butter, melted and cooled slightly

Preheat oven to 350°.
Place apples in an ungreased 13x9-inch baking pan. Mix ¾ cup sugar and
½ teaspoon cinnamon in a small bowl; sprinkle over apples.

Mix flour, 2 cups sugar, ¼ teaspoon cinnamon, baking powder and salt in a
bowl until blended. Add eggs and vanilla; beat with an electric mixer on
medium speed until coarse crumbs form, about 2 minutes. Sprinkle mixture
over apples. Pour melted butter evenly over top. Bake 40–50 minutes or
until apples are tender and top is slightly browned. Refrigerate leftovers.

Makes 10 servings.

APPLE-CRANBERRY COBBLER

This delicious dessert is filled with apples, cranberries and pecans. Serve warm with vanilla ice cream.

Filling
4 large, tart red cooking apples, peeled, cored and sliced
1 12-ounce bag fresh cranberries, cleaned
2 cups brown sugar, packed
1 cup chopped pecans, toasted
1 teaspoon ground cinnamon
⅛ teaspoon ground cloves
1 teaspoon pure vanilla extract

Topping
1 cup all-purpose flour
¾ cup granulated sugar
⅛ teaspoon salt
¼ cup butter, softened
1 egg, beaten
½ teaspoon pure vanilla extract

Preheat oven to 400°.
Grease a 2-quart glass casserole.

Filling: Mix all filling ingredients in prepared casserole.

Topping: Mix flour, sugar and salt in a bowl. Cut in butter with a pastry blender until crumbly. Stir in egg and vanilla until blended. Sprinkle over filling. Bake 25–30 minutes and top is golden. Cool slightly. Refrigerate leftovers.

Makes 8 servings.

APPLE DUMPLING COBBLER

Refrigerated crescent roll dough is used for this apple cobbler.

1 8-ounce can refrigerated crescent rolls
2 large Granny Smith apples, peeled, cored and quartered
1 cup fresh orange juice
⅔ cup granulated sugar
½ cup butter
1 teaspoon pure vanilla extract

2 teaspoons granulated sugar mixed with 1 teaspoon
  ground cinnamon

Preheat oven to 350°.
Lightly grease a 13x9-inch baking dish.

Unroll crescent rolls and separate. Wrap each apple quarter with crescent roll dough; place in prepared baking dish.

Bring orange juice, ⅔ cup sugar and butter to a boil in a saucepan; stir well. Remove from heat; stir in vanilla. Pour mixture over dumplings.

Sprinkle dumplings with sugar-cinnamon mixture. Bake about 25 minutes or until golden and bubbly.

Makes 8 servings.

CAKE MIX APPLE COBBLER

Serve warm with a dollop of whipped cream.

Crust
1 18.25-ounce package moist yellow cake mix
1 cup quick-cooking oatmeal
1 cup chopped walnuts
¾ cup butter, melted

Filling
7 cups peeled, cored and sliced apples
½ cup raisins
½ cup water
3 tablespoons granulated sugar
2 teaspoons ground cinnamon
½ teaspoon ground nutmeg
1 teaspoon pure vanilla extract

Preheat oven to 350°
Grease and flour a 13x9-inch baking pan.

Crust: Mix all crust ingredients in a large bowl until well blended. Sprinkle half the mixture into prepared pan.

Filling: Mix all filling ingredients except vanilla in a saucepan. Cook over low heat 10 minutes, stirring occasionally. Stir in vanilla. Spread filling over crust in pan. Sprinkle remaining crust mixture over filling. Bake about 35 minutes or until lightly browned. Refrigerate leftovers.

Makes 12 servings.

GINGERBREAD APPLE COBBLER

Gingerbread mix is used in this cobbler. Serve warm with ice cream.

1 14-ounce package gingerbread mix, divided
¾ cup water

¼ cup brown sugar, packed
½ cup butter, divided
½ cup chopped pecans

2 21-ounce cans apple pie filling
1 teaspoon pure vanilla extract

Preheat oven to 375°.
Grease an 11x7-inch glass baking dish.
Stir 2 cups gingerbread mix and water in a bowl until smooth; set aside.

In another bowl, stir remaining gingerbread mix with brown sugar; cut in ¼ cup butter with a pastry blender until crumbly. Stir in pecans; set aside.

Cook apple pie filling and remaining ¼ cup butter in a large saucepan over medium heat, stirring constantly, until thoroughly heated. Remove from heat; stir in vanilla. Spoon hot apple mixture evenly into prepared dish. Spoon gingerbread mixture evenly over hot mixture. Sprinkle top with pecan mixture. Bake 30–35 minutes or until set.

Makes 8 servings.

CAKE MIX APPLE CRUMBLE

Top this tasty crumble with sweetened whipped cream.

1 18-ounce package moist white cake mix
½ cup quick-cooking oatmeal
⅓ cup butter, softened
1 teaspoon ground cinnamon
1 tablespoon apple juice or water
1 egg

1 21-ounce can apple pie filling
1 tablespoon fresh lemon juice
1 teaspoon pure vanilla extract

1 cup chopped pecans or walnuts
½ cup quick-cooking oatmeal

Preheat oven to 350°.
Grease a 13x9-inch baking pan.

Beat first six ingredients in a large bowl on low speed until crumbly.
Reserve 1 cup crumb mixture in a small bowl; set aside. Press remaining
mixture into prepared pan. Bake about 15 minutes or until light brown.

Mix apple pie filling, lemon juice and vanilla in a medium bowl; spoon evenly
over hot crust.

Mix pecans and ½ cup oatmeal with reserved crumb mixture; sprinkle over
apple filling. Bake 35 minutes or until light brown. Refrigerate leftovers.

Makes 12 servings.

GRANNY SMITH APPLE CRUMBLE

Serve warm in small bowls topped with vanilla ice cream.

4 pounds large Granny Smith apples, peeled, halved, cored
   and each half cut into 6 slices
2 tablespoons fresh lemon juice
1 teaspoon pure vanilla extract
2 teaspoons ground cinnamon
½ cup granulated sugar

2½ cups old-fashioned oatmeal
1 cup all-purpose flour
1 cup brown sugar, packed
1 cup cold butter, cut up

Preheat oven to 375°.
Butter a 13x9-inch glass baking dish.

Mix apples, lemon juice, vanilla, cinnamon and granulated sugar in a bowl; spoon into prepared baking dish.

Mix oatmeal, flour and brown sugar in a bowl. Cut in butter with a pastry blender until moist clumps are formed. Sprinkle over apple mixture. Bake 45–55 minutes or until apples are tender and topping is brown. Cool slightly before serving. Refrigerate leftovers.

Makes 10 servings.

RHUBARB-APPLE CRUMBLE

Serve warm with sweetened whipped cream.

3 cups peeled, cored and sliced Golden Delicious apples
2 cups diced rhubarb
1 teaspoon pure vanilla extract

½ cup all-purpose flour
½ cup brown sugar, packed
⅓ cup quick-cooking oatmeal
½ teaspoon ground cinnamon
¼ teaspoon salt
¼ cup butter or margarine

Preheat oven to 375°.
Mix apples and rhubarb in a shallow, ungreased 2-quart glass baking dish; drizzle with vanilla.

Mix flour, sugar, oatmeal, cinnamon and salt. Cut in butter with a pastry blender until crumbly. Spoon over apple mixture. Bake 25–30 minutes or until apples are tender. Cool slightly before serving. Refrigerate leftovers.

Makes 6 servings.

APPLE CRISP

Apple crisp is one of my favorite desserts to prepare. I like to use a combi-nation of apples, such as Granny Smith and Golden Delicious.

6 cups apples, peeled, cored and sliced
2 tablespoons granulated sugar
1 teaspoon pure vanilla extract

1 cup brown sugar, packed
¾ cup uncooked old-fashioned oatmeal
¾ cup all-purpose flour
1 teaspoon ground cinnamon
½ teaspoon salt
½ cup cold butter, cut up

Preheat oven to 375°.
Place sliced apples in an ungreased 8x8-inch square glass baking dish; sprinkle with granulated sugar and drizzle with vanilla.

Mix brown sugar, oatmeal, flour, cinnamon and salt in a medium bowl. Cut in butter with a pastry blender until crumbly; sprinkle mixture over apples. Bake 30–35 minutes or until apples are tender and topping is golden brown. Serve warm with vanilla ice cream.

Makes 6 servings.

APPLE-CHERRY CRISP

Serve warm or at room temperature.

3 large Granny Smith apples, peeled, cored and sliced
3 large Cortland apples, peeled, cored and sliced
¾ cup all-purpose flour, divided
¾ cup brown sugar, packed, divided
¾ cup tart dried cherries
½ cup apple cider or apple juice
½ teaspoon ground cinnamon
6 tablespoons butter, cut up

Preheat oven to 350°.
Mix apples, 1 tablespoon flour, 2 tablespoons brown sugar and cherries in a large bowl. Spoon into a shallow, buttered 2-quart baking dish. Pour apple cider over mixture.

Mix remaining flour, remaining brown sugar and cinnamon until well blended; cut in butter with a pastry blender until crumbly. Sprinkle over apples.

Bake 50–55 minutes or until apples are tender and top is browned. Cool on a wire rack. Refrigerate leftovers.

Makes 8 servings.

CRANBERRY-APPLE CRISP

Adapted from my book **The Joy of Cranberries**.

4 Golden Delicious apples, peeled, cored and coarsely chopped
2 cups fresh cranberries
1 cup granulated sugar
1½ teaspoons fresh lemon juice
½ teaspoon pure vanilla extract

1 cup quick-cooking oatmeal
½ cup all-purpose flour
1 cup pecans, coarsely chopped
½ cup butter, melted
⅓ cup brown sugar, packed

Preheat oven to 350°.
Mix apples and cranberries in a greased 11x7x2-inch baking dish. Sprinkle with sugar, lemon juice and vanilla.

Mix remaining ingredients in a bowl; sprinkle over fruit. Bake 1 hour or until golden. Serve warm with vanilla ice cream. Refrigerate leftovers.

Makes 8 servings.

MARY DOW'S APPLESAUCE CRISP

Serve warm with vanilla ice cream…good cold too.

2 cups sweetened applesauce
¼ cup broken pecans
¼ cup broken walnuts
¼ cup chopped salted peanuts
½ cup dark raisins
1 teaspoon pure vanilla extract
½ teaspoon ground cinnamon
½ cup brown sugar
⅛ teaspoon ground nutmeg

Topping
½ cup granulated sugar
1 cup prepared biscuit mix
¼ cup cold butter, cut into small pieces

Preheat oven to 400°.
Mix first nine ingredients in a bowl until blended. Pour mixture into a lightly buttered 9-inch glass pie plate.

Mix granulated sugar and biscuit mix until blended in a medium bowl. Cut in butter with a pastry blender or two knives until crumbly. Sprinkle over applesauce mixture. Place tin foil under pie plate to catch any drips. Bake 30 minutes. Cool 20 minutes before serving. Refrigerate leftovers.

Makes 8 servings.

MICROWAVE APPLE CRISP

A quick dessert…serve with vanilla yogurt or whipped topping.

¾ **cup quick-cooking oatmeal**
¼ **cup all-purpose flour**
¼ **cup brown sugar**
½ **teaspoon ground cinnamon**
½ **teaspoon ground nutmeg**
2 **tablespoons butter or margarine**

4 **apples, peeled cored and thinly sliced**
¼ **cup dried cranberries or raisins**

Mix oatmeal, flour, sugar, cinnamon and nutmeg in a bowl. Cut in butter with a pastry blender until crumbly; set aside.

Mix apples and cranberries in a lightly buttered 8x8-inch microwave-safe dish. Sprinkle with oatmeal mixture. Microwave on high for 12 minutes. Serve hot.

Makes 4 servings.

Cakes
Coffeecakes
Cheesecakes

APPLE UPSIDE-DOWN CAKE

Serve with sweetened whipped cream or vanilla ice cream.

1 cup brown sugar, packed
6 tablespoons butter
¼ cup apple juice
3 tablespoons light corn syrup
¼ teaspoon salt

4 large apples, such as Braeburn,
    peeled, cored and sliced lengthwise
1 tablespoon fresh lemon juice
1½ teaspoons ground cinnamon
¼ teaspoon ground nutmeg

1 18-ounce package moist
    yellow cake mix
¾ cup water
⅓ cup corn oil
3 eggs
1 teaspoon pure vanilla extract
1 teaspoon ground cinnamon
1 large apple, such as
    Braeburn, peeled, cored
    and diced

Preheat oven to 350°.
Grease bottom and sides of a 13x9-inch baking dish.

Mix first five ingredients in a saucepan; bring to a boil over medium heat, stirring until butter is melted; boil 1 minute. Pour caramel mixture into prepared dish.

Toss sliced apples with lemon juice 1½ teaspoons cinnamon and nutmeg in a bowl. Arrange apples over caramel mixture.

Mix cake mix, water, corn oil, eggs, vanilla and 1 teaspoon cinnamon with an electric mixer on low speed until moistened. Beat 2 minutes on medium speed. Fold in diced apples by hand. Pour over sliced apples. Bake about 60–70 minutes or until a wooden pick inserted in center comes out clean. Top will be browned. Cover with a baking sheet and immediately invert. Scrape remaining sauce onto apples. Cool before cutting.

Makes 12 servings.

AUTUMN SURPRISE CAKE

This apple cake recipe comes from my friend, Pam Johnson, of Bloomington, Minnesota. Thanks for sharing a delicious treat.

4 cups cored, unpeeled chopped apples
2 cups granulated sugar
2 teaspoons pure vanilla extract

1 teaspoon salt
1 cup corn oil
2 eggs, beaten

2 cups all-purpose flour
2 teaspoons baking soda
3 teaspoons ground cinnamon
½ cup coconut
1 cup butterscotch-flavored chips
¾ cup chopped nuts

Preheat oven to 350°.
Grease a 13x9-inch baking pan.

Mix apples, sugar and vanilla in a large bowl. Let stand until juice forms. Stir in salt, oil and eggs.

Sift flour, baking soda and cinnamon together; stir into apple mixture. Add coconut; mix well. Pour into prepared baking pan. Sprinkle with butterscotch chips and nuts. Bake 40 minutes or until a wooden pick inserted in center comes out clean. Cool on a wire rack. Store in refrigerator. (Cake will become moist in refrigerator).

Makes 12 servings.

CAKE MIX APPLESAUCE BUNDT CAKE

Sprinkle cooled cake with powdered sugar when serving.

**1 18-ounce package moist butter yellow cake mix
  (or yellow cake mix)**
3 large eggs
1⅛ cups applesauce
½ cup butter, melted
1 teaspoon pure vanilla extract
1 teaspoon ground cinnamon
¼ teaspoon ground nutmeg

½ cup chopped walnuts or pecans

Preheat oven to 375°.
Grease and flour a 10-inch bundt or tube pan.

Beat all ingredients except nuts in a large bowl with an electric mixer on low speed until moistened. Beat on medium speed for 4 minutes. Stir in walnuts by hand. Pour into prepared pan. Bake 45–55 minutes or until a wooden pick inserted in center comes out clean. Cool in pan 25 minutes. Remove from pan; cool completely on a serving plate before serving.

Makes 12 servings.

CARAMEL APPLE PUDDING CAKE

Granny Smith apples are a good choice for this cake.

½ cup butter, softened
½ cup brown sugar, packed
1 large egg
1 teaspoon pure vanilla extract

2½ cups all-purpose flour
1½ teaspoons baking soda
1½ teaspoons ground cinnamon
¼ teaspoon ground nutmeg
¼ teaspoon ground cloves
½ teaspoon salt

1 cup dark corn syrup
1 cup cold water

2 cups peeled and cored apples, finely chopped
½ cup chopped pecans
¾ cup brown sugar, packed
1½ cups boiling water
⅓ cup butter, melted

Preheat oven to 350°.
Beat ½ cup butter and ½ cup brown sugar in a large bowl with an electric mixer on medium speed until creamy. Beat in egg and vanilla.

Mix flour, soda, cinnamon, nutmeg, cloves and salt in a medium bowl; gradually beat into creamed mixture alternately with corn syrup and cold water on low speed, beating well after each addition.

Place apples and pecans in an ungreased 13x9-inch baking pan. Pour batter over top; sprinkle with ¾ cup brown sugar. Mix boiling water and melted butter in a medium bowl. Gently pour over top of batter. Bake 40–50 minutes or until a wooden pick inserted in center comes out clean. Serve warm. Refrigerate leftovers.

Makes 15 servings.

CARAMEL-GLAZED APPLE POUND CAKE

Serve a slice of this caramel-glazed pound cake with cinnamon ice cream or sweetened whipped cream.

Cake
2 cups granulated sugar
1½ cups corn oil
2 teaspoons pure vanilla extract
3 eggs
3 cups all-purpose flour
1 teaspoon baking soda
1 teaspoon salt
2 cups peeled, cored and finely chopped apples
1 cup chopped pecans or walnuts

Glaze
½ cup butter
½ cup brown sugar, packed
2 teaspoons whole milk

Preheat oven to 350°.
Grease and flour a 12-cup bundt pan.

Cake: Beat sugar, corn oil, vanilla and eggs in a large bowl with an electric mixer on medium speed until light and fluffy.

Mix flour, soda and salt in another bowl; stir into creamed mixture until smooth. Stir in apples and pecans. Pour into prepared pan. Bake 60–80 minutes or until a wooden pick inserted in center comes out clean. Cool in pan 20 minutes. Remove from pan; place on a wire rack. Spoon glaze over warm cake.

Glaze: Bring all glaze ingredients to boil in a 2-quart saucepan, stirring occasionally. Boil 2 minutes, stirring constantly. Remove from heat.

Makes 12 servings.

CARAMEL-TOPPED APPLE CAKE

Serve warm with a scoop of vanilla ice cream…and more caramel topping, of course!

1 18-ounce package moist yellow cake mix, divided
1 cup chopped pecans or walnuts
⅓ cup brown sugar, packed
¼ cup butter, softened
¾ teaspoon ground cinnamon
⅛ teaspoon ground cloves

⅓ cup water
2 tablespoons corn oil
2 eggs, lightly beaten
½ teaspoon pure vanilla extract

3 Granny Smith apples, peeled, cored and sliced
½ cup purchased caramel topping

Preheat oven to 350°.
Grease and flour a 13x9-inch baking pan.

Mix 1 cup cake mix, pecans, brown sugar, butter, cinnamon and cloves in a medium bowl until crumbly; set aside.

Stir remaining cake mix, water, corn oil, eggs and vanilla in another bowl until just blended; pour batter into prepared pan; spread evenly.

Place apple slices over batter. Sprinkle with half of the crumbly mixture. Drizzle with caramel topping. Sprinkle with remaining crumbly mixture. Bake 45–50 minutes or until cake pulls away from sides of pan and is golden brown. Cool slightly in pan before serving. Refrigerate leftovers.

Makes 12 servings.

CREAM CHEESE-FROSTED APPLE CAKE

Home-made and delicious.

Cake
½ cup butter, melted
2 cups granulated sugar
2 large eggs
1 teaspoon pure vanilla extract

2 cups all-purpose flour
1 teaspoon baking soda
1 teaspoon salt
2 teaspoons ground cinnamon

4 Granny Smith apples, peeled, cored and sliced
1 cup chopped walnuts, toasted

Frosting
1 8-ounce package cream cheese, softened
3 tablespoons butter, softened
1½ cups powdered sugar
1 teaspoon pure vanilla extract

Preheat oven to 350°.
Grease a 13x9-inch baking pan.

Cake: Mix first four ingredients in a large bowl until blended.

Mix next four ingredients in another bowl until blended, then stir into first mixture until well blended. Stir in apples and walnuts. Spread batter into prepared pan. Bake about 45 minutes or until a wooden pick inserted in center comes out clean. Cool completely in pan on a wire rack.

Frosting: Beat cream cheese and butter with an electric mixer in a bowl until creamy. Gradually beat in sugar until blended. Stir in vanilla. Spread frosting on completely cooled cake. Refrigerate leftovers.

Makes 12 servings.

FUDGE NUT APPLESAUCE CAKE

Cake mix makes this an easy dessert to prepare…applesauce makes it moist and delicious.

1 18-ounce package
    chocolate fudge cake mix
½ cup corn oil
2 eggs
1 cup applesauce

½ cup semisweet chocolate chips
⅓ cup sweetened condensed milk

½ cup milk chocolate chips
½ cup coarsely chopped pecans
powdered sugar

Preheat oven to 350°.
Grease and flour bottom of a 13x9-inch baking pan.

Beat cake mix and corn oil in a large bowl on medium speed 2 minutes. Remove 1 cup of mixture; set aside. Beat eggs and applesauce into remaining mixture on medium speed 3 minutes. Pour into prepared pan; spread evenly.

Place semisweet chocolate chips and sweetened condensed milk in a microwave-safe bowl; microwave uncovered on medium power until chocolate chips are softened, about 1 minute. Stir until smooth. Drop by teaspoonfuls over batter.

Stir milk chocolate chips and pecans into reserved cake mixture; sprinkle over batter. Bake 45–55 minutes or until center is set. Loosen cake from side of pan with a thin knife. Cool completely in pan before serving. When cool, sprinkle lightly with powdered sugar. Refrigerate leftovers.

Makes 12 servings.

LEMON-APPLE CAKE

Serve this simple dessert with whipped topping.

1 21-ounce can apple pie filling
1 teaspoon pure vanilla extract
1 18.25-ounce package lemon cake mix

Preheat oven to 350°.
Grease a 13x9-inch baking pan.

Spread pie filling into prepared pan; drizzle with vanilla extract.
Prepare cake mix as directed on package. Spread evenly over pie filling.
Bake 40–45 minutes or until a wooden pick inserted center comes out
clean. Cool in pan before cutting.

Makes 12 servings.

MINNESOTA APPLE PUDDING CAKE

Apple pudding cake and cream…a delicious affair.

Cake
1⅓ cup granulated sugar
⅔ cup vegetable shortening
2 eggs
2 cups all-purpose flour
2 teaspoons baking soda
2 teaspoons ground cinnamon
1 teaspoon ground nutmeg
6 cups peeled and chopped apples
1 cup chopped pecans, toasted

Sauce
1½ cups brown sugar, packed
2 tablespoons all-purpose flour
¼ cup butter
1 teaspoon pure vanilla extract
1 cup water

Preheat oven to 325°.
Grease a 13x9-inch baking pan.

Cake: Beat granulated sugar and shortening in a large bowl with an electric mixer until creamy. Beat in eggs, one at a time.

Mix flour, baking soda, cinnamon and nutmeg in another bowl until blended. Gradually add to creamed mixture, beating well after each addition. Fold in apples and pecans by hand (mixture will be thick). Spread into prepared pan; top with sauce.

Sauce: Stir brown sugar and flour in a medium saucepan. Stir in butter, vanilla and water. Bring to a boil, stirring occasionally. Boil gently 3 minutes, stirring often. Immediately pour hot sauce over batter. Do not stir. Bake 1 hour. Serve warm with sweetened whipped cream. Refrigerate leftovers.

Makes 12 servings.

SANDRA'S FRESH APPLE CAKE

This apple cake is delicious served warm or cold.

1 cup vegetable oil
2 cups granulated sugar
3 eggs

2½ cups all-purpose flour
1 teaspoon baking soda
2 teaspoons baking powder
1 teaspoon salt

1 teaspoon pure vanilla extract
3 cups peeled and cored chopped apples
1 cup chopped pecans

Preheat oven to 350°.
Grease and flour a tube pan.

Cream oil and sugar in a large bowl. Add eggs; beat well. Mix flour, baking soda, baking powder and salt in a bowl; sift into creamed mixture. Stir in vanilla, apples and pecans (mixture will be very thick). Pour into prepared pan. Bake 55–60 minutes or until a wooden pick inserted in center comes out clean. Cool in pan 15 minutes then remove from pan; cool on a rack.

Makes 12 servings.

SAUERKRAUT APPLE CAKE

Different and delicious!

Cake
1 cup granulated sugar
½ cup brown sugar, packed
4 eggs
1 14-ounce can sauerkraut, rinsed and drained and squeezed dry
1 large Granny Smith apple, peeled, finely grated and squeezed dry
1 cup corn oil
1 cup chopped walnuts
1 teaspoon pure vanilla extract
2 cups all-purpose flour
2 teaspoons baking powder
1 teaspoon baking soda
1 teaspoon salt
2 teaspoons ground cinnamon
½ teaspoon ground nutmeg

Frosting
1 8-ounce package cream cheese
2 tablespoons cream
1 teaspoon pure vanilla extract
4½ cups powdered sugar
½ teaspoon ground cinnamon
1 tablespoon freshly grated
  orange peel

Preheat oven to 350°.
Grease and flour two 8-inch round cake pans, then line with waxed paper.

Cake: Beat sugars and eggs in a large mixing bowl. Stir in sauerkraut, apple, oil, nuts and vanilla. Mix dry ingredients in another bowl; stir into first mixture. Pour batter into prepared pans. Bake 35–40 minutes or until a wooden pick inserted in center comes out clean. Cool in pan 10 minutes, then invert onto a wire rack and cool completely.

Frosting: In a bowl, beat cream cheese, cream and vanilla until fluffy. Beat in powdered sugar until fluffy and spreadable, then beat in cinnamon and orange peel. Refrigerate until ready to use. Spread frosting between cake layers, on top and sides. Refrigerate leftovers.

Makes 12 servings.

SPICY APPLE CAKE

A favorite dessert to take along on a picnic.

Cake
½ cup butter, softened
¾ cup granulated sugar
¾ cup brown sugar, packed
1 cup buttermilk, mixed with
  2 teaspoons baking soda
2 eggs
1 teaspoon pure vanilla extract

2¼ cups all-purpose flour
½ teaspoon salt
1 teaspoon ground cinnamon
¾ teaspoon ground nutmeg
⅛ teaspoon ground cloves
2 cups peeled, cored and finely
  chopped apples

Topping
½ cup chopped pecans
¼ cup granulated sugar
¼ cup brown sugar, packed
¼ teaspoon ground cinnamon

Preheat oven to 350°.
Grease and flour a 13x9-inch baking pan.

Cake: Beat butter and sugars in a large bowl on medium speed until creamy. Add buttermilk mixture, eggs and vanilla.

Mix flour, salt and spices in medium bowl; add to moist ingredients and beat on medium speed until well blended. Stir in apples by hand. Spoon batter into prepared pan.

Topping: Mix all topping ingredients in a small bowl. Sprinkle over batter. Bake 30–35 minutes or until a wooden pick inserted in center comes out clean. Cool in pan on a wire rack.

Makes 15 servings.

STREUSEL APPLE LOAF CAKE

Streusel apple cake…perfect for that afternoon coffee.

Cake
2 cups all-purpose flour
¾ cup granulated sugar
2 teaspoons baking powder
½ teaspoon salt
2 eggs, slightly beaten
½ cup butter, melted and cooled
½ cup whole milk
1 teaspoon pure vanilla extract
2 tart apples, such as Granny Smith, peeled, cored and diced

Streusel
1 cup all-purpose flour
½ cup brown sugar, packed
½ cup butter, melted
2 teaspoons ground cinnamon
⅛ teaspoon ground cloves

Preheat oven to 350°.
Grease a 9x5x3-inch loaf pan.

Cake: Mix flour, sugar, baking powder and salt in a large bowl until well blended. Stir eggs, butter, milk and vanilla in a medium bowl until blended. Fold in the flour mixture with a spatula until just moistened.

Streusel: Mix all streusel ingredients in a medium bowl until crumbly.

Spoon half the cake batter into prepared pan; spread evenly. Top with half the apples, then sprinkle with half the streusel. Top with remaining batter and remaining apples, then sprinkle with remaining streusel. Bake for 70–80 minutes or until a wooden pick inserted in center comes out clean. Cool in pan on a wire rack 10 minutes. Run a thin knife around sides of pan. Remove from pan; cool completely on a wire rack, streusel side up.

Makes 8 servings.

APPLE CREAM CHEESE COFFEECAKE

Serve warm for a special breakfast treat.

1 8-ounce package cream cheese, softened
1 cup granulated sugar
⅓ cup butter
2 eggs
1 teaspoon almond or vanilla extract

1¾ cups all-purpose flour
1 teaspoon baking powder
½ teaspoon baking soda
¼ teaspoon salt
¼ cup whole milk

4 cups Granny Smith apples, peeled, cored and sliced
2 teaspoons fresh lemon juice
½ cup granulated sugar
2 tablespoons all-purpose flour
1 teaspoon ground cinnamon

Preheat oven to 350°.
Grease and flour a 13x9-inch baking pan.

In a large bowl, beat cream cheese, sugar, butter, eggs and almond extract until blended.

In another bowl, mix 1¾ cups flour, baking powder, baking soda and salt; add to first mixture alternately with milk. Pour batter into prepared pan.

Sprinkle apples with lemon juice in a bowl. Mix 2 tablespoons flour and cinnamon in a cup; add to apples and toss to coat. Place apple slices on top of batter.

Bake 50–60 minutes or until a wooden pick inserted near center comes out clean. Let rest a few minutes before cutting into serving pieces.

Makes 12 servings.

APPLE WALNUT COFFEECAKE

Pecans may be substituted for walnuts if desired.

2 cups all-purpose flour
1 cup granulated sugar
1 teaspoon baking powder
1 teaspoon baking soda
¼ teaspoon salt

½ cup dairy sour cream
½ cup butter, softened
¼ cup whole milk
2 eggs
1 teaspoon pure vanilla extract

2 cups cored, peeled and
   chopped apples, such as
   Winesap or Haralson

Topping
½ cup walnuts
½ cup brown sugar, packed
2 tablespoons butter, melted
1 teaspoon ground cinnamon

Preheat oven to 350°.
Grease a 13x9-inch baking pan.

Mix the first five ingredients in a large bowl until blended. Add next five
ingredients. Beat on medium speed, scraping bowl often, until smooth. Stir
in apples by hand. Spread batter into prepared pan.

Mix all topping ingredients in a small bowl; sprinkle over batter. Bake
30–35 minutes or until a wooden pick inserted in center comes out clean.
Cool slightly before cutting.

Makes 12 servings.

PECAN STREUSEL COFFEECAKE

Yogurt and apples in this coffee cake...serve warm.

1 tablespoon butter, melted
1 tablespoon brown sugar, packed
¼ teaspoon ground cinnamon

2 Golden Delicious apples, cored
and sliced

½ cup butter
½ cup granulated sugar
2 eggs
1 teaspoon pure vanilla extract

2 cups all-purpose flour
1 teaspoon baking powder
1 teaspoon baking soda
½ teaspoon salt

1 8-ounce carton plain yogurt

Streusel
¼ cup granulated sugar
1 tablespoon all-purpose flour
1 teaspoon ground cinnamon
¼ cup chopped pecans
1 tablespoon butter, melted

Preheat oven to 350°.
Mix 1 tablespoon melted butter, brown sugar and cinnamon in a 9-inch
square baking pan; spread evenly, then layer with apple slices.

In a bowl, beat ½ cup butter and ½ cup granulated sugar until creamy. Beat
in eggs one at a time; add vanilla.

In another bowl, mix flour, baking powder, baking soda and salt. Add to
creamed mixture alternately with yogurt. Spread half the batter over apple
slices. Mix all streusel ingredients and sprinkle streusel over batter in pan.
Spread with remaining batter.

Bake 30–35 minutes or until a wooden pick inserted near center comes
out clean. Invert onto a serving plate.

Makes 6 servings.

APPLE CHEESECAKE

Top with sweetened cinnamon whipped cream when serving.

Crust
1 cup graham cracker crumbs
½ cup finely chopped pecans
3 tablespoons granulated sugar
¼ cup butter, melted

Filling
2 8-ounce packages cream cheese,
   softened
½ cup granulated sugar
1 teaspoon pure vanilla extract
2 eggs

Topping
⅓ cup granulated sugar
½ teaspoon ground cinnamon
4 cups thinly sliced peeled
   apples
¼ cup finely chopped pecans

Preheat oven to 325°.
Crust: Mix all crust ingredients in a bowl; press onto bottom of a 9-inch springform pan. Bake 10 minutes.

Filling: Beat cream cheese, sugar and vanilla on medium speed until well blended. Beat in eggs, one at a time on low speed. Pour over crust.

Topping: Mix all topping ingredients in a bowl; spoon over cheese layer.

Bake About 70 minutes or until center is almost set. Run a knife around rim of pan to loosen cake. Cool, then remove rim. Refrigerate. Chill well before serving. Refrigerate leftovers.

Makes 12 servings.

BAKED APPLE CHEESECAKE

Top with sweetened whipped cream when serving.

4 cups peeled, cored and sliced Golden Delicious apples

Crust
⅓ cup granulated sugar
⅓ cup butter or margarine
1 tablespoon solid vegetable shortening
¼ teaspoon pure vanilla extract
1 cup all-purpose flour
⅛ teaspoon salt

Filling
2 8-ounce packages cream cheese, softened
½ cup granulated sugar
1 teaspoon pure vanilla extract
2 eggs
1 teaspoon ground cinnamon, mixed with ⅓ cup granulated sugar
¼ cup sliced almonds

Preheat oven to 400°.
Arrange apple slices in a single layer in a shallow baking pan. Cover with cooking foil. Bake 15 minutes; set aside.

Crust: Beat sugar, butter, shortening and vanilla in a bowl with an electric mixer until blended. Stir in flour and salt until crumbly. Pat onto bottom of a 9-inch springform pan; set aside.

Filling: Beat cream cheese, sugar and vanilla with an electric mixer in a bowl until fluffy. Beat in eggs until just combined. Pour onto prepared crust. Arrange warm apple slices over cheese filling. Sprinkle with cinnamon-sugar mixture and sliced almonds.

Bake 40 minutes or until filling is set. Cool to room temperature, then refrigerate. Chill well before serving. Remove side of pan before cutting or serving. Refrigerate leftovers.

Makes 12 servings.

Bars
Squares
Cookies

APPLE CHEESECAKE BARS

A special treat.

1½ cups oatmeal
¾ cup all-purpose flour
½ cup light brown sugar, packed
¼ cup granulated sugar
¾ cup butter-flavored vegetable
   shortening

2 8-ounce packages cream cheese,
   softened
2 large eggs
½ cup granulated sugar
1 teaspoon pure vanilla extract

1 cup peeled, cored and chopped
   Granny Smith apples
½ cup golden raisins
1 teaspoon vanilla extract
½ teaspoon ground cinnamon
¼ teaspoon ground nutmeg
¼ teaspoon ground allspice

Preheat oven to 350°.
Grease a 13x9-inch baking pan.

Mix oats, flour, brown sugar and ¼ cup granulated sugar in a large bowl.
Cut in shortening until crumbly; reserve 1 cup crumb mixture. Press
remaining mixture onto bottom of prepared pan. Bake 12–15 minutes until
set, but do not brown.

Beat cream cheese, eggs, ½ cup granulated sugar and 1 teaspoon vanilla
in another bowl until creamy. Spread over crust.

Mix remaining ingredients in another bowl, then spoon over cream cheese
mixture. Sprinkle reserved crumb mixture evenly over top. Bake 20–25
minutes or until top is golden. Cool completely before cutting into bars.
Store in refrigerator.

Makes 18 bars.

COCONUT APPLE BARS

Coconut and apples paired in this good bar.

1½ cups all-purpose flour
½ teaspoon baking powder
½ teaspoon salt
½ cup butter
1 egg, slightly beaten, mixed with ⅓ cup whole milk

4 cups peeled, cored and thinly sliced Golden Delicious apples
½ cup brown sugar, packed, mixed with ½ teaspoon ground cinnamon

1½ cups shredded coconut
½ cup granulated sugar
1 egg beaten
¼ cup heavy cream
1 teaspoon pure vanilla extract
⅛ teaspoon salt

Preheat oven to 425°.
Mix flour, baking powder and ½ teaspoon salt in a large bowl. Cut in butter
with a pastry blender until crumbly. Add egg and milk mixture; stir with a fork
to form a ball. Knead dough on a lightly floured surface until smooth; place
dough in a 15x10x¾-inch baking pan. Arrange apples over dough in overlapping rows. Sprinkle with brown sugar mixture.

Mix remaining ingredients in a small bowl; spread over top. Bake 20 minutes,
then reduce heat to 350° and continue baking 20 minutes. Cool; cut into
bars. Refrigerate leftovers.

Makes 40 bars.

FROSTED APPLE BARS

This recipe comes from Cambridge, Minnesota...thanks, Kathy.

2½ cups all-purpose flour
1 tablespoon granulated sugar
1 teaspoon salt

1 cup vegetable shortening
2 egg yolks plus enough milk to measure ⅔ cup

10 medium apples, peeled, cored and thinly sliced
1½ cups granulated sugar, mixed with 1¼ teaspoon ground cinnamon
2 egg whites

1 cup powdered sugar
3–4 teaspoons water

Preheat oven to 350°.
Mix first three ingredients in a medium bowl. Cut in shortening. Stir in egg yolk mixture to form dough. Roll out half the dough on a lightly floured surface; place into a 15x10x1-inch jelly roll baking sheet.

Arrange apple slices evenly over dough. Sprinkle with sugar-cinnamon mixture. Roll out remaining half of dough; place over apples. Pinch two ridges of crust to seal. Beat egg whites in a small bowl until frothy; brush lightly over crust. Bake 1 hour.

Whisk powdered sugar with water and drizzle cooled bars with frosting. Refrigerate leftovers.

Makes 48 bars.

GRANNY SMITH APPLE CARAMEL BARS

If you like caramel apples, try making this bar.

1 cup brown sugar, packed
½ cup butter, softened
¼ cup solid shortening
1¾ cups all-purpose flour
1½ cups quick-cooking oatmeal
½ teaspoon baking soda
1 teaspoon salt

4 cups Granny Smith apples, peeled, cored and coarsely chopped
3 tablespoons all-purpose flour
½ teaspoon pure vanilla extract
1 14-ounce bag caramels, melted

Preheat oven to 400°.
Mix sugar, butter and shortening in a large bowl until blended. Stir in 1¾ cups flour, oatmeal, soda and salt. Reserve 2 cups mixture; set aside. Press remaining mixture into an ungreased 13x9-inch baking pan.

Mix apples, 3 tablespoons flour and vanilla; spoon over crumbly mixture. Pour melted caramels over apples. Sprinkle with reserved mixture; press down lightly. Bake 25–30 minutes or until apples are tender and topping is lightly browned. Cool slightly, then cut into bars. Refrigerate leftovers.

Makes 36 bars.

LEMON-GLAZED APPLE BROWNIE

Walnuts and white chocolate in a lemon-glazed blonde apple brownie.

½ cup butter, softened
2 tablespoons margarine
1½ cups brown sugar
2 eggs
2 teaspoons pure vanilla extract
1 tablespoon fresh lemon juice
4 ounces good quality white
  chocolate, melted (not vanilla chips)

2¼ cups all-purpose flour
2 teaspoons baking powder
¼ teaspoon salt
¼ teaspoon nutmeg
1 cup peeled, cored and chopped apples
1 cup walnuts, very coarsely chopped

Glaze
1 cup powdered sugar
1 tablespoon butter, softened
1 teaspoon vanilla extract
1 teaspoon fresh lemon juice
¼ teaspoon grated lemon rind
2 tablespoons hot water

Preheat oven to 350°.
Grease a 13x9-inch baking pan.

Beat butter, margarine and sugar in a medium bowl until light. Beat in eggs, vanilla and lemon juice. Stir in melted chocolate.

Mix flour, baking powder, salt and nutmeg in another bowl; stir into creamed mixture. Stir in apples and chopped walnuts. Spread batter into prepared pan. Bake 30–35 minutes. Cool in pan on a rack.

Stir all glaze ingredients to a smooth drizzle consistency and glaze brownies. Refrigerate leftovers.

Makes 24 brownies.

LOLA'S APPLESAUCE BARS

Applesauce bars…a delicious treat to offer with that afternoon coffee.

1 cup granulated sugar
2 tablespoons butter or margarine, softened
½ cup regular applesauce
1 egg, beaten
1 teaspoon pure vanilla extract

1 cup chunky applesauce
⅓ cup dark raisins
1 tablespoon light brown sugar, packed
¾ teaspoon ground cinnamon

1½ cups all-purpose flour
¾ cup quick-cooking oatmeal
1 teaspoon baking powder
½ teaspoon salt

Preheat oven to 375°.
Grease an 8x8-inch square baking pan.

Beat granulated sugar and butter in a large bowl with an electric mixer on medium speed until creamy. Stir in regular applesauce, egg and vanilla.

Mix flour, oatmeal, baking powder and salt in a medium bowl; stir into creamed mixture until well blended. Spoon half the batter into prepared pan; spread evenly.

Mix chunky applesauce, raisins, brown sugar and cinnamon in a small bowl; spoon evenly over batter. Spread remaining batter evenly over filling. Bake 30–35 minutes or until lightly browned. Cool in pan 15 minutes. Cut into bars. Store leftovers in refrigerator.

Makes 16 bars.

MINNESOTA CREAM CHEESE-FROSTED APPLE-CRANBERRY BARS

Fresh or frozen cranberries may be used in this recipe.

1½ cups granulated sugar
1 cup butter, softened
2 eggs
2 teaspoons freshly grated
   orange peel
2 teaspoon pure vanilla extract

2¼ cups all-purpose flour
1 teaspoon baking powder
¼ teaspoon salt
2 cups peeled, cored and chopped
   apples
1 cup cranberries, coarsely chopped
1 cup chopped pecans or walnuts

Frosting
⅓ cup butter, softened
1 3-ounce package cream
   cheese, softened
1 teaspoon pure vanilla extract
2 cups powdered sugar
1 teaspoon freshly grated
   orange peel
2–4 teaspoons milk

Preheat oven to 350°.
Grease a 15x10x1-inch baking pan.

Beat first five ingredients on medium speed until blended, about 3 minutes. Mix flour, baking powder and salt; beat into first mixture on low speed for 2 minutes. Stir in apples, cranberries and pecans by hand. Spread into prepared pan. Bake 30–35 minutes or until a wooden pick inserted in center comes out clean. Cool completely before frosting.

Frosting: Beat butter, cream cheese and vanilla on medium speed until well blended, about 2 minutes. On low speed, gradually beat in powdered sugar, orange peel and enough milk to make a spreading consistency. Thinly frost, then cut bars. Refrigerate leftovers.

Makes 48 bars.

ZUCCHINI APPLESAUCE BARS

Moist and frosted bars…substitute chopped nuts for raisins if desired.

⅔ cup brown sugar, packed
¼ cup butter, softened
2 eggs
1 teaspoon pure vanilla extract

1 cup all-purpose flour
1 teaspoon baking soda
⅛ teaspoon salt
¾ teaspoon ground cinnamon
½ teaspoon ground cloves

¾ cup applesauce
½ cup shredded zucchini, drained
¾ cup dark raisins

Frosting
1½ cups powdered sugar
2 tablespoons butter, softened
1 teaspoon pure vanilla extract
2–3 tablespoons orange juice
  (approximately)

Preheat oven to 350°.
Grease a 9x9-inch square baking pan.

Beat sugar, butter, eggs and vanilla in a large bowl with an electric mixer
until creamy.

Mix flour, soda, salt, cinnamon and cloves in a small bowl; stir into creamed
mixture. Stir in applesauce, zucchini and raisins. Spread into prepared pan.
Bake 25–35 minutes or until a wooden pick inserted near center comes
out clean. Cool completely in pan.

Frosting: Beat powdered sugar, butter, vanilla and just enough orange juice
with an electric mixer to a smooth consistency. Frost and cut bars. Cover
and refrigerate leftovers.

Makes 16 bars.

BUTTERSCOTCH APPLE SQUARES

Butterscotch, apples and coconut in this square.

¼ cup butter, melted
1½ cups graham cracker crumbs
1¼ cups peeled, cored and chopped apples

1 6-ounce package butterscotch-flavored chips
1 14-ounce can sweetened condensed milk
1⅓ cups flaked coconut
1 cup chopped nuts

Preheat oven to 350°.
Spread butter into a 13x9-inch baking pan. Sprinkle evenly with graham cracker crumbs. Top with apples.

Melt butterscotch chips with sweetened condensed milk in a heavy saucepan over medium heat, stirring constantly. Pour mixture evenly over apples. Top with coconut and then chopped nuts; press down firmly. Bake 25–30 minutes or until lightly browned. Cool, then cut into squares. Refrigerate leftovers.

Makes 12 servings.

CARAMEL APPLE OAT SQUARES

Serve with a scoop of vanilla ice cream

1¾ cups all-purpose flour
1 cup quick-cooking oatmeal
½ cup brown sugar, packed
½ teaspoon baking soda
½ teaspoon salt
¼ teaspoon ground cinnamon

1 cup cold butter or margarine
1 21-ounce can apple pie filling

20 caramels, unwrapped
1 14-ounce can sweetened condensed milk
1 teaspoon pure vanilla extract

1 cup chopped walnuts

Preheat oven to 350°.
Mix first six ingredients in a large bowl until blended. Cut in butter with a pastry blender until crumbly. Reserve 1½ cups mixture; set aside. Press remaining mixture on bottom of a 13x9-inch baking pan. Bake 15 minutes. Spoon pie filling over prepared crust.

Melt caramels with sweetened condensed milk in a heavy saucepan over low heat, stirring until smooth. Stir in vanilla. Spoon over pie filling.

Add walnuts to reserved crumb mixture; spoon over top. Bake about 20 minutes or until set. Cool slightly.

Makes 12 servings.

SAUCY CARAMEL APPLE SQUARES

Serve warm in a shallow dessert bowl with cinnamon whipped cream.

1½ cups all-purpose baking mix
⅔ cup granulated sugar
½ cup whole milk

2 cups peeled, cored and sliced Golden Delicious apples
1 tablespoon fresh lemon juice
1 teaspoon pure vanilla extract

¾ cup brown sugar, packed
½ teaspoon ground cinnamon
1 cup boiling water

Preheat oven to 350°.
Stir baking mix and granulated sugar in a medium bowl until blended. Stir in milk. Pour into an ungreased 9x9-inch square baking pan. Top with apples. Sprinkle with lemon juice and vanilla extract.

Mix brown sugar and cinnamon in a small bowl; sprinkle over apples. Pour boiling water over apples. Bake 50–60 minutes or until a wooden pick inserted in center comes out clean. Cool slightly before serving. Refrigerate leftovers.

Makes 6 servings.

SOUR CREAM APPLE SQUARES

Serve warm with sweetened cinnamon whipped cream.

2 cups all-purpose flour
2 cups brown sugar, packed
½ cup butter, softened
1 cup chopped walnuts

1 teaspoon baking soda
½ teaspoon salt
1 teaspoon ground cinnamon
⅛ teaspoon ground nutmeg
1 8-ounce container dairy sour cream
1 egg
1 teaspoon pure vanilla extract

2 cups peeled, cored and finely chopped Golden Delicious apples

Preheat oven to 350°.
Beat flour, brown sugar and butter in a large mixer bowl with an electric mixer on low speed until crumbly. Stir in walnuts. Measure 2¾ cups crumbly mixture; press into an ungreased 13x9-inch baking pan.

In the same bowl, stir the remaining crumbly mixture with the next seven ingredients until well mixed. Stir in apples. Spoon into baking pan over crumb crust. Bake 30–40 minutes or until a wooden pick inserted in center comes out clean. Cool slightly in pan before cutting into squares. Store covered in refrigerator.

Makes 12 servings.

STREUSEL APPLE SQUARES

Serve warm or at room temperature…with whipped cream, of course.

Streusel
¾ cup all-purpose flour
¾ cup chopped pecans
⅓ cup brown sugar, packed
6 tablespoons butter, slightly softened
¾ teaspoon ground cinnamon
2 teaspoons pure vanilla extract

Crust
2 cups all-purpose flour
¼ cup granulated sugar
¼ teaspoon salt
½ cup cold butter, cut-up

Filling
3 tablespoons butter
2 pounds Golden Delicious apples, peeled, cored and diced
½ cup dark raisins
⅓ cup brown sugar, packed
½ teaspoon ground cinnamon

1 tablespoon cornstarch
2 tablespoons lemon juice
½ teaspoon pure vanilla extract

Preheat oven to 375°.
Lightly grease a 13x9-inch baking pan

Streusel: Mix all streusel ingredients in a bowl, using hands, until well blended; refrigerate mixture while preparing crust and filling.

Crust: Mix flour, granulated sugar and salt in a large bowl. Blend cold cut-up butter with fingertips into flour mixture until fine crumbs are formed. Press into prepared pan. Bake until golden, about 15 minutes.

Filling: Stir butter, apples, raisins, brown sugar and cinnamon in a large skillet over medium heat until apples are tender, about 10 minutes. Mix cornstarch, lemon juice and vanilla until blended; stir into apple mixture until thickened. Spoon over baked crust. Sprinkle streusel over top. Bake about 30 minutes or until browned. Cool completely in pan before cutting into squares. Refrigerate leftovers. Makes 15 servings.

GLAZED APPLE COOKIES

Fresh apples, walnuts and raisins in these glazed cookies.

1⅓ cup brown sugar, packed
½ cup butter or margarine
1 egg
1 teaspoon pure vanilla extract

2 cups all-purpose flour
1 teaspoon baking soda
¼ teaspoon salt
1 teaspoon ground cinnamon
¼ teaspoon ground cloves

¼ cup apple juice
1½ cups chopped unpeeled apples
1 cup chopped walnuts or pecans
1 cup dark raisins

Glaze
1½ cups powdered sugar
1 tablespoon butter, softened
¼ teaspoon pure vanilla extract
1–2 tablespoons orange juice

Preheat oven to 400°.
Beat brown sugar and butter in a bowl with an electric mixer until creamy.
Beat in egg and vanilla.

Mix flour, soda, salt, cinnamon and cloves in a medium bowl; gradually beat into creamed mixture until blended.

Beat in apple juice. Stir in apples, walnuts and raisins by hand. Drop batter by the rounded tablespoonfuls onto greased baking sheets. Bake for 7–8 minutes or until edges are golden brown. Cool on a wire rack.

Beat all glaze ingredients to a spreading consistency and spread over warm cookies.

Makes 3 dozen.

KIKI'S APPLESAUCE COOKIES

Kiki lives in Blaine, Minnesota, and shares her applesauce cookie recipe…thanks, old friend.

1 cup brown sugar
½ cup shortening
1 egg
½ cup applesauce
1 teaspoon pure vanilla extract

1¾ cups all-purpose flour
½ teaspoon baking soda
½ teaspoon salt
1 teaspoon ground cinnamon
¼ teaspoon ground cloves
1 cup raisins

Glaze
¼ cup butter
2 cups powdered sugar
1 teaspoon pure vanilla extract
1–2 tablespoons orange juice (approximately)

Preheat oven to 400°.
Beat first five ingredients in a large bowl until creamy. In another bowl, mix flour, soda, salt, cinnamon and cloves; blend into creamed mixture. Stir in raisins. Cover and refrigerate dough 1 hour.

Drop cookie dough by rounded teaspoonfuls 2 inches apart on an ungreased cookie sheet. Bake until almost no indentation remains when touched, about 8–10 minutes. Remove from baking sheet; cool completely on a rack.

Glaze: Melt butter in a small saucepan. Remove from heat; stir in powdered sugar and vanilla. Add orange juice, a little at a time; beat until a smooth glaze is formed. Glaze cooled cookies.

Makes 2 dozen.

PEANUT BUTTER APPLESAUCE COOKIES

A tasty chewy cookie.

1 cup crunchy peanut butter
1 cup unsweetened applesauce
2½ cups brown sugar, packed
2 egg whites
2 teaspoons pure vanilla extract

3½ cups all-purpose flour
1½ teaspoons baking soda
½ teaspoon salt

Preheat oven to 375°.
Mix first five ingredients in a large bowl until well blended.

Mix flour, soda and salt in another bowl; stir into first mixture until blended.
Drop batter by rounded tablespoonfuls onto baking sheet coated with non-stick cooking spray. Bake 8–10 minutes or until light golden brown.
Remove from baking sheet; cool on a wire rack.

Makes 5 dozen.

SESAME APPLE COOKIES

Sesame seeds and honey in this good cookie.

¾ cup all-purpose flour
¾ cup whole wheat flour
½ cup quick-cooking oatmeal
¼ cup sesame seeds
¼ cup granulated sugar
1 teaspoon baking powder
½ teaspoon baking soda
1 teaspoon ground cinnamon
½ teaspoon ground nutmeg
¼ teaspoon salt

½ cup honey
½ cup corn oil
⅓ cup whole milk
1 large egg

1½ cups peeled, cored and finely
   chopped Golden Delicious apples
¾ cup dark raisins

Preheat oven to 375°.
Mix first ten ingredients in a large bowl until blended.

Beat next four ingredients in a small bowl; blend into dry mixture.

Stir in apples and raisins until combined. Drop batter by tablespoonfuls onto
ungreased baking sheets. Bake 10–12 minutes or until lightly browned.
Remove cookies from baking sheet; cool on a wire rack.

Makes 2 dozen.

Pies

APPLE ALMOND PIE

Top this delicious pie with sweetened whipped cream when serving.

1 9-inch unbaked pie crust

¾ cup slivered almonds, ground
½ cup granulated sugar
2 tablespoons butter, melted and cooled
1 egg

4 cups peeled, cored and sliced Empire or Gala apples
¼ cup granulated sugar
1 teaspoon ground cinnamon
1 tablespoon fresh lemon juice
½ teaspoon pure vanilla extract
¼ cup sliced almonds

Topping
¼ cup apricot preserves
1 tablespoon water
1 tablespoon Grenadine syrup

Preheat oven to 350°.
Place crust in a 9-inch pie plate. Mix ground almonds, ½ cup sugar, butter and egg in a bowl until blended; spread evenly into crust.

Mix apples, ¼ cup sugar, cinnamon, lemon juice and vanilla in a large bowl; spoon filling over almond mixture in crust. Sprinkle with sliced almonds.

Bake about 45 minutes or until apples are tender and crust is golden.

Mix all topping ingredients in a small bowl; spoon evenly over hot filling. Cool completely before serving. Refrigerate leftovers.

Makes 8 servings.

APPLE-BLUEBERRY CHEDDAR CRUMB PIE

Apples with blueberries topped with a cheddar cheese crust.

Filling
3 cups peeled, cored and sliced tart apples
1 cup blueberries
1½ tablespoons cornstarch
1 cup granulated sugar
½ teaspoon ground cinnamon
1 teaspoon pure vanilla extract

Crumb crust
1 cup all-purpose flour
3 tablespoons butter
2 tablespoons granulated sugar
½ cup grated sharp cheddar cheese

Preheat oven to 425°.
Filling: Mix all filling ingredients in a large bowl. Spoon into a 9-inch pie plate. Top with crumb crust mixture. Bake 40–50 minutes. Cool slightly before serving. Store in refrigerator. Serve warm or at room temperature.

Crumb crust: Mix all ingredients in a medium bowl until crumbly.

Makes 8 servings.

APPLE BUTTER PIE

Top with whipped cream when serving.

1 9-inch unbaked pie crust

½ cup apple butter
1 egg, slightly beaten
½ cup granulated sugar
1 tablespoon all-purpose flour
2 cups evaporated milk

ground cinnamon

Preheat oven to 425°.
Mix apple butter, egg, sugar, flour and milk in a bowl until well-blended.
Pour mixture into crust. Sprinkle lightly with cinnamon.

Bake 10 minutes. Reduce heat to 350° and continue baking about 35 minutes or until a knife inserted in center comes out clean. Cool on a wire rack. Refrigerate leftovers.

Makes 8 servings.

APPLE BUTTERMILK CUSTARD PIE

Offer your guests a slice of this apple custard pie for a special treat.

1 9-inch deep dish unbaked pie crust

Filling
1 tablespoon margarine
**5 cups cored, peeled and sliced
  Granny Smith apples**
1 cup granulated sugar, divided
½ teaspoon ground cinnamon
2 tablespoons all-purpose flour
¼ teaspoon salt
3 large eggs
1¾ cups buttermilk
1 teaspoon pure vanilla extract

Streusel
⅓ cup all-purpose flour
⅓ cup brown sugar
½ teaspoon ground cinnamon
2½ tablespoons cold butter

Preheat oven to 325°.
Place crust into a 9-inch deep dish pie plate.

Streusel: Mix all streusel ingredients until crumbly; refrigerate until ready to use.

Filling: Melt margarine in a large nonstick skillet over medium-high heat.
Add sliced apples, ¼ cup granulated sugar and cinnamon. Stir and cook
until apples are tender, about 10 minutes. Spoon into prepared crust.

Whisk ¾ cup granulated sugar, flour, salt and eggs. Stir in buttermilk and
vanilla. Pour over apple mixture. Bake 30 minutes. Reduce heat to 300°.
Sprinkle top of pie with streusel. Bake an additional 40 minutes or until set.
Cool 1 hour on a wire rack before serving. Store in refrigerator.

Makes 10 servings.

APPLE CHESS PIE

Top with sweetened whipped cream when serving.

1 9-inch unbaked pie crust

½ cup butter
½ cup granulated sugar
½ cup brown sugar, packed
¼ teaspoon salt
3 large eggs

2 Golden Delicious apples, cored and chopped
2 tablespoons all-purpose flour
1 teaspoon pure vanilla extract
½ cup sour cream
½ cup chopped pecans

Preheat oven to 425°.
Place pie crust into a 9-inch pie plate. Lightly prick bottom of pie crust with a fork. Bake until lightly browned; set aside.

Reduce heat to 325°.
Beat butter, both sugars and salt in a large bowl using an electric mixer until light and fluffy. Beat in eggs, one at a time.

Stir in remaining ingredients until well mixed. Spoon into baked pie shell. Bake for 50–60 minutes or until lightly browned. Cool completely before serving. Store in refrigerator.

Makes 8 servings.

APPLE-CRANBERRY PIE

Serve warm with vanilla ice cream.

2 9-inch unbaked pie crusts

4 cups apples, peeled, cored and sliced
1½ cups fresh or frozen whole cranberries
¼ cup raisins
1 cup granulated sugar
¼ cup brown sugar
¼ cup all-purpose flour
½ teaspoon ground cinnamon
¼ teaspoon salt
1 teaspoon pure vanilla extract

2 tablespoons cold butter, cut up

Preheat oven to 400°.
Place 1 crust into a 9-inch pie plate. Mix all filling ingredients except butter in a large bowl. Spoon filling into crust. Dot with butter. Cover with top crust. Seal and flute edges; cut slits in top crust.

Bake 50–55 minutes or until apples are tender. Cool on a wire rack.

Makes 8 servings.

APPLE CREAM PIE

Use a mixture of tart apples, such as Granny Smith and Baldwin for this sweet pie.

Crust
1 cup all-purpose flour
½ teaspoon salt
¼ teaspoon ground cinnamon
⅓ cup solid vegetable shortening
3–4 tablespoons cold water, approximately

Filling
6 medium apples, peeled, cored and quartered
1 tablespoon fresh lemon juice
1 teaspoon pure vanilla extract
1 cup brown sugar, packed
¼ cup all-purpose flour
¼ teaspoon ground cinnamon
⅛ teaspoon salt
1 cup whipping cream

Preheat oven to 400°.
Crust: Mix flour, salt and cinnamon in a medium bowl. Cut in shortening until mixture is size of small peas. Sprinkle water, a little at a time, over mixture; toss with a fork until dough is just moist enough to hold together. Form dough into a ball. Flatten dough and roll out on a floured surface to a circle 11/2 inches larger than an inverted 9-inch pie pan. Line a 9-inch pan with crust. Fold edge to form a upright rim; flute. Set aside.

Filling: Place apples in a bowl; toss with lemon juice. Place apples, round side up, in prepared pie crust. Drizzle with vanilla.

Mix brown sugar, flour, cinnamon and salt in a bowl; sprinkle ¾ cup mixture over apples. Pour cream over apples. Sprinkle with remaining brown sugar mixture. Bake at 400° 10 minutes, then reduce heat to 350° and continue baking 45–60 minutes or until apples are tender. Refrigerate leftovers.

Makes 8 servings.

APPLE PECAN UPSIDE-DOWN PIE

Top with vanilla ice cream when serving.

2 9-inch unbaked pie crusts

¼ cup butter or margarine
½ cup pecan halves
⅔ cup brown sugar, packed

6 cups apples, peeled, cored and sliced
2 tablespoons fresh lemon juice, optional
1 teaspoon pure vanilla extract
1 tablespoon all-purpose flour
½ cup granulated sugar
½ teaspoon ground cinnamon
¼ teaspoon salt

Preheat oven to 450°.
Spread butter evenly on bottom and sides of a 9-inch pie pan. Press pecan halves, round side down, onto butter. Sprinkle evenly with brown sugar. Place 1 pie unbaked crust over brown sugar, trim evenly.

Mix remaining ingredients, except remaining pie crust, in a large bowl until apples are coated. Spoon mixture over crust in pie pan, keeping top level. Top with remaining crust. Trim, fold and flute. Prick top of crust with a fork.

Bake for 10 minutes, then reduce heat to 350° and continue baking 35–40 minutes. Remove from oven when syrup stops bubbling. Place a serving plate over pie and carefully invert. Remove pie pan. Cool slightly before serving. Refrigerate leftovers.

Makes 8 servings.

APPLESAUCE PIE

Applesauce pie in a sour cream crust. Serve warm or cold topped with sweetened cinnamon whipped cream.

Crust
1 cup all-purpose flour
1 tablespoon granulated sugar
¼ teaspoon salt
⅓ cup butter-flavored solid vegetable shortening
3 tablespoons dairy sour cream

Filling
¾ cup granulated sugar
¼ cup all-purpose flour
¼ teaspoon ground cinnamon
1½ cups applesauce
¼ cup butter, melted and cooled
3 eggs
1 teaspoon pure vanilla extract

Preheat oven to 425°.
Crust: Mix flour, sugar and salt in a medium bowl; cut in shortening to form coarse crumbs. Stir in sour cream with a fork until particles are moistened and cling together. Form dough into a ball. Flatten dough slightly and roll out on a lightly floured surface or a floured pastry cloth until it's 2 inches larger than an inverted 9-inch pie plate. Place crust into a 9-inch pie plate. Trim and flute edge.

Filling: Mix all filling ingredients in a medium bowl until well blended. Pour into prepared crust.

Bake 10 minutes, then reduce heat to 350° and continue baking 20–30 minutes or until center is set. Cool before serving. Refrigerate leftovers.

Makes 8 servings.

BAKED LITTLE APPLE PIES

Serve these little baked apple pies warm or at room temperature.

Crust
- ⅓ cup hot milk
- ¼ cup solid vegetable shortening
- 1 cup all-purpose flour
- ½ teaspoon salt
- ¼ teaspoon baking powder

Filling
- 1 cup dried apples, chopped
- ½ cup dried cranberries
- ½ cup water
- ½ cup apple cider
- ½ teaspoon pure vanilla extract
- ¼ cup brown sugar, packed

Glaze
- 1 large egg white
- 1 tablespoon water
- 1½ teaspoons granulated sugar

Crust: Mix hot milk and shortening in a large bowl until shortening is dissolved. Mix flour, salt and baking powder in a small bowl; gradually add to milk mixture, tossing with a fork just until blended. Turn dough out onto a piece of plastic food wrap. Knead into a ball (dough will be sticky). Cover and chill at least 2 hours.

Filling: Mix apples, cranberries, water and apple cider in a small saucepan. Bring to a boil over medium-high heat. Reduce heat. Cover and simmer 10 minutes or until fruit is tender, stirring occasionally. Stir in vanilla and brown sugar. Remove from heat. Cool to room temperature.

Preheat oven to 450°.

Crust: Divide chilled dough into 8 equal portions. Work with 1 portion at a time (cover remaining dough to prevent drying). Roll each portion into a 6-inch circle on a lightly floured surface. Spoon about 2 tablespoons filling on half of each circle; moisten edges of dough with water. Fold dough over filling; press edges together with a fork to seal. Place pies on a baking sheet coated with cooking spray.

Glaze: Whisk egg white with water in a small bowl; brush mixture over pies. Sprinkle with granulated sugar. Bake about 12 minutes or until golden. Remove from baking sheet to a wire rack. Refrigerate leftovers. Makes 8 pies.

CARAMEL APPLE CRUMB PIE

Serve with a dollop of whipped topping.

1 9-inch baked pie crust

Filling
1 tablespoon butter
½ cup brown sugar, packed
¾ teaspoon ground cinnamon
⅛ teaspoon salt
9 cups cored, peeled and sliced Granny Smith apples
3 tablespoons all-purpose flour
2 teaspoons fresh lemon juice
1 teaspoon pure vanilla extract
¼ cup prepared caramel ice cream syrup

Topping
¼ cup all-purpose flour
¼ cup brown sugar, packed
2 tablespoons cold butter, cut up

Preheat oven to 375°.
Filling: Melt butter in a large nonstick skillet over medium-high heat. Mix brown sugar, cinnamon and salt in a small bowl; add to skillet. Add apples. Cook and stir 5 minutes. Remove from heat. Stir in flour, lemon juice and vanilla; spoon into prepared crust. Drizzle with caramel syrup.

Topping: Mix all topping ingredients in a bowl until crumbly. Sprinkle over caramel syrup.

Bake about 30 minutes or until apples are tender. Cool on a wire rack. Refrigerate leftovers.

Makes 10 servings.

CRANBERRY-APPLE STREUSEL CUSTARD PIE

Apples and cranberries in custard…topped with a walnut streusel.

1 9-inch unbaked pie crust

Filling
**1½ cups peeled, cored and sliced
  Golden Delicious apples
1½ cups fresh cranberries
1 14-ounce can sweetened
  condensed milk
2 eggs, beaten
½ cup hot water
1 teaspoon pure vanilla extract
1 teaspoon ground cinnamon**

Streusel
**½ cup brown sugar, packed
½ cup all-purpose flour
⅛ teaspoon salt
¼ cup butter, softened
½ cup chopped walnuts**

Preheat oven to 375°.
Place crust into a 9-inch pie plate.

Filling: Mix all filling ingredients in a large bowl until combined; spoon into pie crust.

Streusel: Mix all streusel ingredients except walnuts in a medium bowl until crumbly. Stir in walnuts. Sprinkle mixture over filling.

Bake for 30–40 minutes or until golden brown. Cool slightly, then store covered in refrigerator.

Makes 8 servings.

DEEP DISH APPLE PIE

Deep dish apple pie...look for company!

Crust
⅓ cup solid shortening
1 tablespoon cold butter
1 cup all-purpose flour, mixed
  with ½ teaspoon salt
2–3 tablespoons cold water,
  approximately,

Filling
1½ cups granulated sugar
½ cup all-purpose flour
¾ teaspoon ground cinnamon
½ teaspoon ground nutmeg
¼ teaspoon salt
12 cups cored, peeled and thinly
  sliced Granny Smith apples
1 teaspoon pure vanilla extract
2 tablespoons butter

Preheat oven to 400°.
Crust: Cut shortening and butter into flour with two knives or a pastry blender until small pea-size particles form. Add water, a little at a time, just to moisten, tossing with a fork. Form dough into a ball; flatten slightly. Roll dough out into a 10-inch square on a lightly floured surface with a floured rolling pin; set aside.

Filling: Mix sugar, flour, cinnamon, nutmeg and salt in a large bowl. Add apples; mix well. Spoon into an ungreased 9x9x2-inch square baking pan. Drizzle with vanilla and dot with butter. Top with prepared crust; cut 3 slits on top. Fold crust edges under just inside edges of pan. Bake about 1 hour or until juices begin to flow through slits in crust. Cool slightly before serving with vanilla ice cream. Refrigerate leftovers.

Makes 12 servings.

DOUBLE CRUSTED APPLE PIE

Apple pie…America's favorite dessert.

Crust
- **2 cups all-purpose flour**
- **1 teaspoon salt**
- **⅔ cup solid shortening**
- **1 tablespoons cold butter**
- **4–5 tablespoons ice cold water, approximately**

Filling
- **⅔ cup granulated sugar**
- **¼ cup all-purpose flour**
- **½ teaspoon ground cinnamon**
- **½ teaspoon ground nutmeg**
- **⅛ teaspoon salt**
- **7 cups tart cooking apples, peeled, cored and cut into ¼-inch slices**
- **1 teaspoon pure vanilla extract**
- **2 tablespoons cold butter, cut up**

Preheat oven to 400°.
Crust: Mix flour and salt. Cut in shortening and butter with a pastry blender until mixture resembles coarse crumbs. Stir in water with a fork just until moistened. Divide dough in half; form each into a ball; flatten slightly. Wrap1 ball of dough in plastic food wrap; refrigerate. Roll remaining dough into 12-inch circle on a lightly floured surface with a floured rolling pin. Fold into quarters; place into a 9-inch-pie plate. Unfold dough, pressing firmly against bottom sides. Trim crust to ½ inch from edge of pan; set aside.

Filling: Mix sugar, flour, cinnamon, nutmeg and salt in a large bowl. Stir in apples. Spoon into prepared crust. Drizzle with vanilla and dot with butter.

Roll out refrigerated dough into a 12-inch circle. Fold into quarters; place over filling; unfold. Trim, seal and flute edge. Cut 5 slits in crust. Cover edge of crust with a 2-inch strip of aluminum foil. Bake 35 minutes. Remove aluminum foil. Continue baking about 20 minutes or until crust is lightly browned and juices begin to bubble through slits. Serve warm with vanilla ice cream. Store in refrigerator. Makes 8 servings.

FRIED APPLE PIES

Sprinkle with powdered sugar just before serving.

1 cup cored, peeled and chopped Golden Delicious apples
4 tablespoons orange juice, divided
1 tablespoon granulated sugar
1 teaspoon grated orange peel
pinch salt
2 teaspoons cornstarch
½ teaspoon pure vanilla extract

pastry for one 9-inch pie crust
oil for deep-frying

Mix apples, 3 tablespoons orange juice, sugar, orange peel and salt in a saucepan over medium heat. Cover and simmer until apples are tender, about 10 minutes. Dissolve cornstarch in 1 tablespoon orange juice and vanilla; stir into hot mixture and cook until thickened.

Roll out pastry thinly on a floured surface. Cut into 5-inch rounds. Place 1½ tablespoons of filling on each round. Moisten edges with water. Fold in half. Seal edges well with a fork. Prick a few small holes in top of pies.

Heat oil to 375° in a deep fryer. Fry the pies in hot oil about 3 minutes or until golden brown. Remove with a slotted spatula and drain on paper towels. Refrigerate leftovers.

Makes 6 pies.

GLAZED APPLE-RHUBARB PIE

Apples and rhubarb with a glazed lattice top…country good!

9½-inch double pie crust, unbaked

Filling
**9 cups cored, peeled and sliced
  Granny Smith apples**
**1½ cups tender rhubarb, cut into
  ½-inch pieces**
¾ cup granulated sugar
½ cup light brown sugar, packed
2 tablespoons all-purpose flour
1 tablespoon cornstarch

¾ teaspoon ground cinnamon
¼ teaspoon ground nutmeg
1 teaspoon pure vanilla extract

Glaze
1 egg, beaten
1 tablespoon cold water
1 tablespoon granulated sugar
**1 teaspoon ground pecans or
  walnuts**
⅛ teaspoon ground cinnamon

Preheat oven to 425°.
Place 1 crust into a 9½-inch pie plate.

Filling: Mix apples and rhubarb in a large bowl. Mix granulated sugar, brown sugar, flour, cornstarch, cinnamon and nutmeg in a bowl; sprinkle over apple mixture and toss to coat. Spoon into prepared crust. Drizzle with vanilla. Cut remaining crust into 1-inch-wide strips. Moisten pastry edge with water and cover pie with a lattice top. Flute edge high. Place on a baking sheet to catch any drips.

Glaze: Mix egg and water in a small bowl; brush over top crust. Mix remaining glaze ingredients and sprinkle over crust.

Bake 20 minutes, then reduce heat to 350° and continue baking 30–40 minutes or until filling in center is bubbly and crust golden brown. Cool to room temperature. Serve warm with vanilla ice cream. Refrigerate leftovers.

Makes 8 servings.

IMPOSSIBLE FRENCH APPLE PIE

Almost magic…makes it's own crust!

2 large Golden Delicious apples, peeled, cored and sliced
1 large Granny Smith apple, peeled, cored and sliced
1 teaspoon ground cinnamon
¼ teaspoon ground nutmeg

½ cup all-purpose baking mix
½ cup granulated sugar
½ cup whole milk
1 tablespoon butter or margarine, softened
2 eggs
½ teaspoon pure vanilla extract

Streusel
½ cup all-purpose baking mix
¼ cup chopped nuts
¼ cup brown sugar, packed
2 tablespoons butter

Preheat oven to 325°.
Grease a 9-inch pie plate.
Stir apples, cinnamon and nutmeg in a bowl; spoon into prepared pie plate.

Beat remaining ingredients, except streusel ingredients, in another bowl
until blended; pour over apple mixture.

Streusel: Mix all streusel ingredients until crumbly; sprinkle on top of pie.
Bake 40–50 minutes or until a knife inserted in center comes out clean.
Cool slightly on a rack before serving. Refrigerate leftovers.

Makes 6 servings.

NO-BAKE APPLE PIE

Garnish with whipped topping when serving.

Crust
1½ cups graham cracker crumbs
¼ cup granulated sugar
⅓ cup butter, melted

Filling
4 cups cored, peeled and thinly sliced Granny Smith apples
⅔ cup granulated sugar
¾ cup apple juice
½ teaspoon ground cinnamon
2 tablespoons cornstarch
¼ cup cold water
1 teaspoon pure vanilla extract
1 4-serving size package lemon-flavored gelatin, dry

Crust: Mix all crust ingredients in a bowl until blended. Press mixture onto bottom and sides of a 9-inch pie plate. Chill.

Filling: Mix apples, sugar, apple juice and cinnamon in a medium saucepan; bring to a boil over medium-high heat. Reduce to medium; cook about 5 minutes or until apples are tender. Mix cornstarch and water in a cup; stir into apple mixture. Return to a boil; boil 1 minute, stirring constantly. Remove from heat; stir in vanilla. Stir in gelatin until completely dissolved. Pour mixture into prepared crust. Refrigerate until set. Store in refrigerator.

Makes 8 servings.

PUMPKIN-APPLE PIE

This pie is for those who can't decide...pumpkin or apple? Serve it topped with sweetened whipped cream.

1 9-inch unbaked pie crust

1 cup canned pumpkin puree, not pie mix
⅓ cup brown sugar, packed
1 egg
¼ teaspoon salt
1 teaspoon pumpkin pie spice
1 teaspoon pure vanilla extract
1 5-ounce can evaporated milk

1 21-ounce can apple pie filling
¼ cup chopped pecans
2 tablespoons caramel ice cream topping

Preheat oven to 375°.
Place crust into a 9-inch pie plate.

Beat pumpkin puree, sugar, egg, salt, pumpkin spice, vanilla and milk in a large bowl until smooth. Pour into prepared crust.

Drop apple pie filling by the tablespoonfuls on top of pumpkin mixture. Sprinkle with pecans and drizzle with caramel topping.

Bake about 45 minutes or until filling is set and crust is browned. Cool completely before serving. Store in refrigerator.

Makes 8 servings.

THE BIG APPLE APPLE PIE

New York apple pie…serve it warm with vanilla ice cream.

Crust
½ cup butter, softened
½ cup granulated sugar
1 cup all-purpose flour
¼ cup chopped nuts
¼ teaspoon pure vanilla
 extract

Filling
5 cups peeled, cored and coarsely
 chopped Golden Delicious apples
½ cup raisins
½ cup chopped walnuts, pecans, hazelnuts,
 or a combination of all three
½ cup applesauce
½ teaspoon pure vanilla extract
¼ cup granulated sugar
2 tablespoons all-purpose flour
1 teaspoon ground cinnamon
¼ teaspoon salt

Preheat oven to 400°.
Crust: Beat butter and sugar in a medium bowl with an electric mixer until
blended. Add flour, nuts and vanilla. Mix just until combined. Form dough
into a ball. Pat dough into bottom and 1 inch up the sides of a 9-inch
springform pan. Bake 10 minutes, then set aside while preparing filling.

Filling: Mix all filling ingredients in a large bowl until apples are well coated.
Spoon into the partially baked crust. Bake 40–45 minutes or until apples
are tender. Cool slightly; remove side of pan. Refrigerate leftovers.

Makes 10 servings.

ZUCCHINI-APPLE CREAM PIE

Another delicious way to use zucchini!

1 9-inch deep dish unbaked pie crust

Filling
2 cups peeled, seeded, chopped zucchini
2 cups all-purpose cooking apples, peeled, cored and chopped
1 cup granulated sugar
1 cup evaporated milk, undiluted
1 egg
1 tablespoon soft butter or margarine
3 tablespoons all-purpose flour
¼ teaspoon salt
1 teaspoon pure vanilla extract
¼ teaspoon ground cinnamon
⅛ teaspoon ground nutmeg, or as desired

Preheat oven to 400°.
Place crust into a 9-inch deep dish pie plate.

Filling: Cook zucchini in a small amount of water in a large saucepan over medium heat 8 minutes. Add apples; cook 5 minutes. Drain. Put zucchini-apple mixture into a blender. Add remaining ingredients except nutmeg. Blend until smooth; pour into prepared crust. Sprinkle top with nutmeg. Bake 15 minutes, then reduce heat to 350° and bake an additional 30 minutes. Cool slightly. Store in refrigerator.

Makes 8 servings.

Desserts

APPLE BROWN BETTY

When serving, top this old-fashioned dessert with vanilla ice cream or whipped topping.

6 tablespoons butter, melted, divided
2 cups fresh white bread crumbs

3 Granny Smith apples, peeled, cored and sliced ¼-inch thick
2 tablespoons fresh lemon juice
¼ cup brown sugar, packed
¼ teaspoon ground cinnamon
1 tablespoon all-purpose flour
1 teaspoon pure vanilla extract

Preheat oven to 375°.
Grease four 6-ounce ramekins equally with 2 tablespoons melted butter.

Mix remaining 4 tablespoons melted butter with bread crumbs in a small bowl; set aside. Mix remaining ingredients in a large bowl until apples are well coated.

Divide one-third of the bread crumbs equally into prepared ramekins. Then top each equally with half of the apple mixture. Repeat layers with one-third of the bread crumbs and remaining apples, ending with the final one-third of the bread crumbs. Press down firmly on mixture. Bake 20 minutes, then increase heat to 450° and continue baking until apples are tender, about 10 minutes. Cool on a wire rack. Remove from ramekins and place on individual dessert plates. Serve warm. Refrigerate leftovers.

Makes 6 servings.

APPLE CHARLOTTE

Serve with sweetened whipped cream or vanilla custard.

4 tablespoons butter
6 pounds peeled, cored and thinly
    sliced tart-sweet apples
zest of 1 fresh lemon
2 tablespoons fresh lemon juice
¾ cup granulated sugar
1 vanilla bean, split in half lengthwise

1 loaf firm white bread (about
    10 slices) crust removed
6 tablespoons melted butter

Melt 4 tablespoons butter in a large saucepan over medium heat. Add apples, lemon zest, lemon juice, sugar and vanilla bean. Cook and stir until apples are very soft. Reduce heat to low and continue cooking, stirring often, 15 minutes. Remove from heat; set aside. Discard vanilla bean.

Preheat oven to 400°.
Place a round of buttered parchment paper in the bottom of a 1-quart charlotte mold or ovenproof bowl with a flat bottom. Cut 4 slices of bread in half to form triangles, and then cut triangles in half. Brush one side with melted butter; place buttered side down in prepared mold. Cut remaining slices into strips that are 1 inch wide and long enough to reach the top of the mold; brush with butter, and arrange buttered side out in an upright fashion, overlapping slightly, along the sides to line the mold completely.

Spoon apple mixture into mold; completely cover mixture with remaining bread pieces. Cut to fit, placing buttered side out. Place mold on a baking sheet. Bake 15 minutes. Reduce heat to 350° and continue baking until bread is golden, about 35 minutes. Cool 15 minutes on a wire rack. Unmold and serve warm. Refrigerate leftovers.

Makes 8 servings.

APPLE CHEDDAR QUESADILLAS

Sprinkle with a little powdered sugar when serving.

⅓ cup granulated sugar
½ teaspoon ground cinnamon
2 cups apples, peeled, cored and thinly sliced
⅓ cup raisins
½ teaspoon rum extract
8 6-inch flour tortillas
1½ cups shredded low-fat cheddar cheese

In a small bowl, mix sugar and cinnamon; reserve 1 tablespoon mixture. Spray a large skillet with butter-flavored nonstick cooking spray. Add apples; cook and stir over medium heat until tender. Stir in sugar mixture (except the reserved amount), raisins and extract. Top each tortilla evenly with cheese to within ½ inch of edge. Spread apple mixture over cheese.

Spray a medium nonstick skillet with cooking spray; heat until hot over medium heat. Place 1 tortilla in skillet, filling side up; heat 1 minute. Remove from skillet and immediately fold in half. Cover and keep warm; continue making remaining quesadillas.

Cut each into 3 wedges. Sprinkle with reserved sugar-cinnamon mixture.

Makes 24 servings.

APPLE CRÈME BRÛLÉE

Crème brûlée…an elegant dessert.

3 Granny Smith apples, cored, peeled and cut into bite-size chunks
1 tablespoon ground cinnamon
¼ cup granulated sugar
¼ cup water

6 egg yolks
6 tablespoons granulated sugar
1 teaspoon pure vanilla extract
1½ cups heavy whipping cream
extra granulated sugar

Preheat oven to 325°.
Stir and cook apples, cinnamon, ¼ cup sugar and water in a saucepan over medium heat until tender but not mushy, about 7 minutes. Set aside; cool.

Whisk egg yolks and 6 tablespoons sugar until light yellow. Add vanilla. Gradually whisk in whipping cream.

Divide apples evenly into 6 ungreased ramekins. Top evenly with cream mixture. Place ramekins in a baking dish. Pour hot water into baking dish until it reaches halfway up the sides of ramekins. Bake until set, about 40 minutes. Remove from oven, but keep ramekins in water bath 30 minutes. Remove ramekins from water bath; refrigerate and chill 8 hours.

When serving, sprinkle granulated sugar on top of crème and carefully torch until golden brown. Refrigerate leftovers.

Makes 6 servings.

APPLE CUSTARD ENCHILADAS

Custard filled apple enchiladas...not just for kids!

Custard
1½ cups milk
2 tablespoons cornstarch
¼ cup granulated sugar
⅛ teaspoon salt
1 egg
½ teaspoon pure vanilla extract

Filling
**2 tablespoons sweetened dried
 cranberries, chopped**

¼ cup boiling water
1 tablespoon butter
**1 pound Golden Delicious apples,
 peeled, cored and sliced**
¾ teaspoon ground cinnamon, divided
⅛ teaspoon ground nutmeg
2 tablespoons dark brown sugar

2 tablespoons water
½ teaspoon granulated sugar
8 6-inch flour tortillas

Preheat oven to 350°.
Custard: Bring milk to a boil in a small saucepan. Mix cornstarch, sugar, salt and egg in a small bowl until blended. Stir a small amount of hot milk into cornstarch mixture, and quickly stir back into milk until blended. Cook and stir over medium-low heat until thickened, about 6 minutes. Remove from heat; stir in vanilla. Reserve ⅓ cup custard for garnish.

Filling: Mix cranberries and boiling water in a bowl; let stand to plump; set aside. Melt butter in a 10-inch saucepan over medium heat. Add apples, ½ teaspoon cinnamon and nutmeg. Cook, stirring occasionally, until softened, about 8 minutes. Stir in brown sugar; cook until mixture is slightly thickened. Remove from heat. Drain cranberries; stir half into apple mixture.

Mix 2 tablespoons water and granulated sugar; brush tortillas with mixture. Fill each tortilla with ¼ cup apple mixture; spoon 2 tablespoons custard over apple mixture. Roll up tortillas; place seam side down in a lightly greased 11x7-inch glass baking dish. Sprinkle with remaining cinnamon. Cover tightly with cooking foil. Bake 10–12 minutes or until light golden brown. Garnish with reserved custard and remaining cranberries; serve warm. Refrigerate leftovers. Makes 8 servings.

APPLE DUMPLINGS

Serve this comfort dessert warm in a small bowl with plain sweet cream or sweetened cinnamon whipped cream.

Pastry
2 cups all-purpose flour
1 teaspoon salt
¾ cup solid vegetable shortening
5 tablespoons cold water, approximately

Filling
6 baking apples, such as Rome Beauty, cored
3 tablespoons dark seedless raisins
3 tablespoons chopped walnuts
½ teaspoon ground cinnamon, divided
½ cup granulated sugar
½ cup dark corn syrup
1 cup water
2 tablespoons butter
1 teaspoon pure vanilla extract

Preheat oven to 425°.
Pastry: Mix flour and salt in a medium bowl. Cut in shortening with a pastry blender until small particles are formed. Add water, a little at a time, stirring with a fork until flour is just moistened. Form dough into a ball. Roll dough out on a lightly floured surface. Cut dough into six 4-inch squares.

Filling: Place an apple on each pastry square. Mix raisins, walnuts and ¼ teaspoon cinnamon in a small bowl. Fill apples equally with mixture. Moisten corners of pastry squares with a little water, and bring 2 opposite corners up over apple; pinch to seal. Repeat with other 2 corners. Place dumplings in an ungreased 11x7x2-inch baking dish.

Stir sugar, corn syrup, water, butter and ¼ teaspoon cinnamon in a medium saucepan. Bring to a boil; boil 3 minutes. Stir in vanilla and pour around dumplings. Bake 45 minutes or until apples are tender, basting with syrup from baking dish several times during cooking period. Refrigerate leftovers.

Makes 6 servings.

APPLE FLAN

This recipe comes from Houston, Texas...thanks, cousin Jane.

1¼ cups whole milk
⅔ cup granulated sugar, divided
3 eggs
1 teaspoon pure vanilla extract
¼ teaspoon salt, divided
⅔ cup all-purpose flour

2½ cups fresh apple slices
2 tablespoons butter, cut up
powdered sugar

Preheat oven to 350°.
Mix milk, ⅓ cup granulated sugar, eggs, vanilla, ⅛ teaspoon salt and flour in a medium bowl; beat until smooth and creamy. Spread about ½ cup batter into a 9-inch pie plate. Bake 6–7 minutes or until batter begins to set.

Arrange apple slices over batter; sprinkle with remaining granulated sugar and salt. Dot with butter. Pour remaining batter over apples. Return to oven and continue baking about 50 minutes or until browned and slightly puffed. Sprinkle with powdered sugar as desired. Refrigerate leftovers.

Makes 6 servings.

APPLE KUCHEN

All-purpose baking mix makes this an easy dessert to prepare.

2 cups all-purpose baking mix
⅔ cup whole milk
¼ cup granulated sugar
2 tablespoons corn oil
1 egg

1 8-ounce package cream cheese, softened
¼ cup granulated sugar
1 egg
½ teaspoon pure vanilla extract
1½ cups thinly sliced peeled and cored apples

3 tablespoons sugar mixed with ¼ teaspoon ground cinnamon

Preheat oven to 350°.
Grease and flour a 13x9-inch baking pan.

Stir baking mix, milk, ¼ cup sugar, corn oil and egg in a bowl until well mixed. Pour into prepared pan.

Beat cream cheese, ¼ cup sugar, egg and vanilla until well blended. Spread over batter. Top with sliced apples. Sprinkle with sugar-cinnamon mixture. Bake 35–40 minutes. Refrigerate leftovers.

Makes 10 servings.

APPLE LASAGNA

Cheese and apples in this sweet lasagna.

8 lasagna noodles
2 cups shredded cheddar cheese
1 cup ricotta cheese
1 egg, lightly beaten
¼ cup granulated sugar
1 teaspoon almond extract

2 20-ounce cans apple pie filling

1 cup dairy sour cream
⅓ cup brown sugar, packed
6 tablespoons all-purpose flour
6 tablespoons brown sugar, packed
¼ cup quick-cooking oatmeal
½ teaspoon ground cinnamon
⅛ teaspoon ground nutmeg
3 tablespoons margarine

Preheat oven to 350°.
Grease a 13x9-inch baking pan.

Cook lasagna noodles following package directions. Drain in a colander.
Mix cheddar cheese, ricotta cheese, egg, granulated sugar and almond
extract in a medium bowl until well blended.

Spread 1 can apple pie filling onto bottom of prepared pan. Layer half the
noodles over filling; spread cheese mixture over noodles. Top with the
remaining noodles, then remaining can of pie filling.

Mix sour cream with ⅓ cup brown sugar; refrigerate.

Mix flour, 6 tablespoons brown sugar, oatmeal, cinnamon and nutmeg in a
small bowl. Cut in margarine until crumbly; sprinkle mixture over apple pie
filling. Bake 45 minutes. Cool 15 minutes. Cut into squares; garnish with
sour cream mixture. Refrigerate leftovers.

Makes 12 servings.

APPLE PANDOWDY

Use a purchased crust or make your own; either will work in this pandowdy.

1 9-inch unbaked pie crust

Filling

**3 pounds Cortland apples,
   peeled, cored and cut
   into ½-inch-thick slices**
1 tablespoon fresh lemon juice
1 teaspoon pure vanilla extract
½ cup granulated sugar

¼ cup brown sugar, packed
2 tablespoons all-purpose flour
½ teaspoon ground cinnamon
¼ teaspoon ground nutmeg
¼ teaspoon salt
1½ tablespoons cold butter, cut up

Preheat oven to 400°.
Filling: Mix all filling ingredients, except butter, in a large bowl until well combined. Pour into a lightly buttered 9x9-inch square baking dish. Dot with butter.

Roll out unbaked crust on a lightly floured surface into a 10-inch square; place over apples. Tuck dough in and down around the edges. Cut several slits on top to vent steam.

Bake 40 minutes. Cut crust into 2-inch squares with a knife and push some of the pieces down into apple juices. Return to oven and continue baking until filling is bubbling and crust is golden brown, about 15–20 minutes. Cool slightly before serving. Serve warm with vanilla ice cream. Refrigerate leftovers.

Makes 8 servings.

APPLE SORBET

A refreshing dessert.

4 Golden Delicious apples, peeled, cored and sliced
½ cup granulated sugar
¼ cup water

1½ teaspoons fresh lemon juice
½ teaspoon pure vanilla extract
¼ teaspoon ground cinnamon

Place apples, sugar and water in a medium saucepan. Cover and simmer until apples are tender, about 15 minutes. Cool. Puree mixture in food processor or blender until smooth.

Stir in remaining ingredients. Pour into an 8x8-inch square nonreactive baking pan. Cover and freeze until almost firm, about 1–2 hours. Spoon into a large bowl and beat with an electric mixer until light and foamy. Return to pan and freeze until firm. Store in freezer.

Makes about 2½ cups.

APPLE STRUDEL

Sprinkle lightly with powdered sugar when serving.

Filling
**3 Golden Delicious apples, peeled,
cored and very thinly sliced**
1 tablespoon fresh lemon juice
1 teaspoon pure vanilla extract
½ cup chopped walnuts
½ cup golden raisins
2 tablespoons granulated sugar

Crumb mix
2 tablespoons plain bread crumbs
2 tablespoons granulated sugar
1 teaspoon ground cinnamon
½ teaspoon grated lemon zest
1 tablespoon butter, melted

Pastry
**4 sheets 12x17-inch frozen puffed
pastry, thawed**
½ cup melted butter

Preheat oven to 400°.
Lightly grease a baking sheet.

Filling: Toss all filling ingredients in a large bowl; set aside.

Crumb mix: Mix crumbs, sugar, cinnamon and lemon zest in a small bowl.
Add melted butter; toss until combined. Set aside.

Pastry: Stack two sheets of puffed pastry on a clean kitchen tea towel.
Brush each all over with melted butter. Top with 2 more sheets, and brush
each with butter. Sprinkle with crumb mix, then spread with apple filling
along one short end. Using the tea towel to help you, carefully roll pastry
jelly-roll style. Place seam-side down on prepared baking sheet. Brush with
melted butter. Make 2 small slits on top to vent steam. Bake for 25–30
minutes or until golden brown and apples are tender. Cool at least 15
minutes before serving. Refrigerate leftovers.

Makes 10 servings.

BAKED APPLES

Nothing beats the aroma of cinnamon spiced apples baking in the oven. Serve warm with whipped cream or vanilla ice cream.

6 baking apples such as Ida Red or Rome Beauty

Filling
12 tablespoons brown sugar, packed, or granulated sugar
6 teaspoons butter
¾ teaspoon ground cinnamon
vanilla

Preheat oven to 375°.
Core apples. Peel a ½-inch strip around middle of each apple. Place apples standing upright in an ungreased baking dish.

Mix all filling ingredients and divide equally among centers of apples. Drizzle a few drops of pure vanilla over top of each.

Add water to baking dish to cover bottom ¼-inch deep. Bake uncovered for 30–40 minutes, basting with syrup in dish several times while baking, until apples are tender when pierced with a fork. Refrigerate leftovers.

Makes 6 servings.

CARAMEL APPLE DESSERT

Serve warm with cinnamon whipped cream.

1½ cups all-purpose baking mix
⅔ cup granulated sugar
½ cup whole milk
2 cups peeled, cored and sliced Golden Delicious apples
1 tablespoon fresh lemon juice
1 teaspoon pure vanilla extract
¾ cup brown sugar, packed
½ teaspoon ground cinnamon
1 cup boiling water

Preheat oven to 350°.
Stir baking mix and granulated sugar in a medium bowl. Stir in milk. Pour mixture into an ungreased 9x9-inch square baking pan. Top with apples. Sprinkle with lemon juice and vanilla. Mix brown sugar and cinnamon in a small bowl; sprinkle over apples. Pour boiling water over apples. Bake 50–60 minutes or until a wooden pick inserted in center comes out clean. Cool slightly before serving. Refrigerate leftovers.

Makes 6 servings.

CARAMEL APPLE SHORTCAKES

Use purchased caramel sauce instead of homemade, if desired.

Shortcakes
2½ cups all-purpose baking mix
3 tablespoons granulated sugar
½ cup whole milk
4 tablespoons butter, melted,
  divided
¼ cup chopped pecans
2 tablespoons brown sugar
¼ teaspoon ground cinnamon

Caramel sauce
3 cups granulated sugar
1 cup water
2 cups whipping cream

Filling
1 tablespoon butter
5 Gala apples, peeled, cored and sliced
½ cup apple juice
3 tablespoons brown sugar
¼ teaspoon ground cinnamon
sweetened whipped cream

Preheat oven to 375°.

Shortcakes: Stir baking mix, granulated sugar, milk and 3 tablespoons butter until a soft dough forms. Knead dough on a lightly floured surface until smooth. Pat dough to a ¼-inch thickness. Cut with a 2¾-inch biscuit cutter. Place on lightly greased baking sheet. Mix pecans, brown sugar, cinnamon and remaining tablespoon butter in a bowl; place on top of biscuits. Bake 12–15 minutes or until browned.

Caramel sauce: Stir granulated sugar with water in a saucepan; bring to a boil and cook 15–20 minutes without stirring, or until it is caramel colored. Swirl mixture around pan until it turns golden amber in color. Remove from heat. Gradually add cream, stirring constantly with a long-handled wooden spoon. If caramel starts to harden, return to low heat and stir until smooth.

Filling: Melt butter in a large saucepan over medium-high heat. Add apples; toss to coat. Stir in juice, sugar and cinnamon. Bring to a boil; reduce heat to low; simmer 10–15 minutes or until apples are tender. Pour ½ cup caramel sauce over apples; toss.

Split shortcakes in half. Layer half of biscuit halves with apple mixture and sweetened whipped cream.top with remaining biscuit halves. Drizzle with remaining caramel sauce. Refrigerate leftovers. Makes 12 servings.

CHEDDAR STUFFED BAKED APPLES

You'll love the aroma coming from the kitchen when these apples are in the oven…serve warm.

8 Golden Delicious apples

1 cup apple juice or orange juice
½ teaspoon pure vanilla extract
¼ cup brown sugar, packed
½ teaspoon ground cinnamon

4 ounces shredded sharp cheddar cheese
¼ cup raisins
¼ cup chopped pecans, toasted

Preheat oven to 350°.

Remove cores from apples to within ½-inch of bottoms of apples; pierce skins with a sharp knife. Place apples in a lightly buttered shallow baking dish.

Mix juice, vanilla, sugar and cinnamon in a bowl; pour over apples.

Bake 30–35 minutes or until apples are tender, basting occasionally with juice mixture. Mix cheese, raisins and pecans in a small bowl; spoon evenly into center of apples. Let stand 1 minute. Refrigerate leftovers.

Makes 8 servings.

CREAMY APPLE RICOTTA BREAD PUDDING

Serve with warm caramel dessert topping.

1 15-ounce container ricotta cheese
2 cups whole milk
2 eggs
¾ cup granulated sugar

8 slices cinnamon raisin bread, cubed
1 large Golden Delicious apple, peeled, cored and chopped
1 teaspoon pure vanilla extract

2 tablespoons granulated sugar mixed with ⅛ teaspoon
   ground cinnamon

Preheat oven to 350°.
Beat cheese with a wire whisk in a large bowl until smooth. Add milk, eggs
and ¾ cup sugar; beat with whisk until well blended.

Add bread cubes, apples and vanilla to cheese mixture; gently stir until
bread is moistened. Pour into a shallow, greased 3-quart baking dish. Bake
45–50 minutes or until center is almost set. Sprinkle with sugar-cinnamon
mixture. Serve warm. Refrigerate leftovers.

Makes 8 servings.

MICRO-BAKED APPLES

Other large apples such as Gala may be used.

4 large Fuji apples
4 teaspoons butter or margarine, divided
¼ cup dried cranberries, divided
¼ cup maple syrup

Remove core from apples, but do not cut through to bottom. Beginning at the stem end, peel apple one-third of the way down. Stand apples in an 8x8-inch glass microwave-safe dish. Fill each apple with 1 teaspoon butter and 1 tablespoon cranberries. Pour maple syrup over and around apples.

Cover with vented plastic food wrap and cook on medium-high (70% power) for 10–11 minutes or until apples are very tender. Let stand, covered, for 5 minutes. Serve warm with ice cream. Refrigerate leftovers.

Makes 4 servings.

PECAN APPLE DUMPLINGS WITH SAUCE

Pecan-filled apple dumplings, topped with a delicious sauce.

Dumplings
2 cups all-purpose flour
¼ teaspoon salt
½ cup cold butter
⅔ cup dairy sour cream
**6 medium tart cooking apples,
   cored and peeled**

⅓ cup granulated sugar
⅓ cup chopped pecans
¼ teaspoon ground cinnamon
2 tablespoons butter, softened
whole milk

Sauce
½ cup brown sugar, packed
½ cup whipping cream
2 tablespoons butter
1 teaspoon pure vanilla extract

Preheat oven to 400°.
Dumplings: Mix flour and salt in a medium bowl; cut in cold butter until crumbly. Stir in sour cream with a fork until mixture forms into a dough. Roll dough into a 18x12-inch rectangle on a lightly floured surface. Cut into six 6-inch squares. Place an apple in center of each square.

Mix sugar, pecans, cinnamon and softened butter. Fill center of each apple with 1½ tablespoons mixture. Fold dough up around apple; seal seams well. Place on a greased 15x10x1-inch jelly-roll baking pan, seam-side down. Brush dough with milk, and prick with a fork. Bake 35–45 minutes or until apples are fork-tender. Cover with aluminum cooking foil if crust browns too fast.

Sauce: Mix all sauce ingredients in a small saucepan. Cook over medium heat, stirring occasionally, until mixture comes to a full boil, about 3–4 minutes. Serve warm sauce over warm dumplings. Refrigerate leftovers.

Makes 6 servings.

STEAMED APPLE PUDDING

Steamed apple pudding…a fall favorite.

Hard sauce
¼ cup butter, softened
2 tablespoons apple juice
½ teaspoon pure vanilla extract
1½ cups powdered sugar
⅛ teaspoon ground nutmeg

Pudding
¼ cup butter
½ cup brown sugar, packed
1 large egg
⅓ cup maple syrup

1¾ cups all-purpose flour
1 teaspoon baking powder
½ teaspoon baking soda
⅛ teaspoon salt
1 teaspoon ground cinnamon
½ teaspoon ground ginger
½ cup buttermilk
1 cup cored, peeled and chopped
  Golden Delicious apple

Hard sauce: Beat butter and juice for 1 minute. Beat in rest of sauce ingredients until smooth. Refrigerate until firm.

Grease an ovenproof 6-cup lidded metal pudding mold; dust with powdered sugar; set aside.

Pudding: Beat butter, brown sugar, egg and syrup. Beat in remaining ingredients except apples, scraping bowl often, until blended. Stir in apples. Spoon into prepared mold. Clamp on lid. If mold does not have a lid, cover tightly with double thickness of heavy-duty cooking foil. Pour 1 inch of water in a Dutch oven. Place filled mold on a rack in Dutch oven. Cover.

Cook over high heat until water boils. Reduce heat. Cook at a very slow boil over low heat 2–2½ hours, or until a wooden pick inserted in center of pudding comes out clean. If more water is needed during steaming, quickly lift cover and add boiling water. Be very careful.

Remove mold from Dutch oven. Remove foil. Allow steam to escape before inverting pudding onto a serving plate. Serve with a wedge of hard sauce. Refrigerate leftovers. Makes 6 servings.

WALNUT APPLE CREAM CHEESE DESSERT

When serving, top with warm caramel sauce.

2 cups all-purpose flour
1 cup brown sugar, packed
½ cup granulated sugar
1 teaspoon ground cinnamon

½ cup butter
1 cup chopped walnuts

1 8-ounce package cream cheese, softened
2 tablespoons whole milk
¼ cup granulated sugar
1 egg, beaten
1 teaspoon pure vanilla extract
4 cups peeled, cored and chopped Golden Delicious apples

Preheat oven to 350°.
Mix first four ingredients in a medium bowl. Cut in butter with a pastry blender until crumbly. Stir in walnuts. Reserve 2 cups mixture. Press remaining mixture onto bottom of an ungreased 13x9x2-inch baking pan.

Beat cream cheese and milk in a bowl with an electric mixer until well blended. Stir in ¼ cup sugar, egg and vanilla until well blended. Pour over crust. Top with apples. Sprinkle with reserved crumb mixture. Bake 30–40 minutes or until crust is golden and apples are tender. Cool slightly, then store in refrigerator. Cut into squares.

Makes 12 servings.

Tarts
Tortes

APPLE-CRANBERRY PECAN TART

A delicious tart. Garnish with whipped cream when serving.

pastry for 10-inch single pie crust

Filling
1¼ cup unsweetened apple juice, divided
1⅛ cups granulated sugar
**3 Granny Smith apples, cored, peeled
    and cubed**
1 12-ounce package fresh cranberries
½ cup all-purpose flour
1 teaspoon pure vanilla extract

Topping
⅓ cup chopped pecans
⅓ cup all-purpose flour
3 tablespoons butter, melted
¼ cup brown sugar, packed
24 pecan halves

Preheat oven to 450°.
Fit pastry into an 11-inch fluted tart pan with removable bottom. Cover with heavy-duty cooking foil. Bake 5 minutes. Remove foil, and continue baking about 7 minutes or until nearly done. Cool in pan.

Filling: Bring ¾ cup apple juice and granulated sugar to a boil over medium heat, stirring often. Add apples and cranberries; return to a boil. Reduce heat and simmer uncovered until apples are tender and cranberries pop, about 6 minutes. Stir flour and ½ cup apple juice in a small bowl until smooth; stir into apple mixture. Bring to a boil; cook and stir 2 minutes. Remove from heat; cool to room temperature and spoon into cooled crust.

Topping: Mix chopped pecans, flour, butter and brown sugar in a bowl until crumbly; sprinkle over filling. Place pecan halves forming two circles over filling. Bake in a preheated 375° oven 30–35 minutes or until golden brown. Cool on a wire rack. Refrigerate leftovers.

Makes 12 servings.

APPLE TART

Top with toasted chopped pecans and vanilla ice cream when serving.

Crust
- **1¼ cups all-purpose flour**
- **¼ cup granulated sugar**
- **½ teaspoon salt**
- **10 tablespoons butter, cut up**
- **1 egg yolk, beaten with**
  - **1 tablespoon cold water**

Filling
- **2 egg yolks**
- **6 tablespoons granulated sugar, divided**
- **1 tablespoon cornstarch**
- **½ teaspoon pure vanilla extract**
- **⅓ cup whipping cream**
- **⅓ cup frozen apple juice concentrate, thawed**
- **3 tablespoons butter**
- **3 large Golden Delicious apples, peeled, cored and sliced**

Crust: Mix flour, sugar and salt in a medium bowl. Cut in butter until mixture resembles coarse meal. Add egg mixture; mix to form a dough. Flatten dough and chill 1 hour. Bring dough to room temperature; press evenly over bottom and up sides of a 9-inch tart pan with removable bottom; trim. Freeze crust 25 minutes. Preheat oven to 400°. Line crust with cooking foil filled with dry beans. Bake 15 minutes. Remove foil and beans. Bake until light golden. Cool completely.

Filling: Whisk yolks, 2 tablespoons sugar, cornstarch and vanilla in a bowl. Bring cream and concentrate to a simmer in a heavy saucepan over medium heat; whisk into egg yolk mixture, then return to same saucepan. Whisk over medium heat until mixture boils and thickens. Pour into a bowl; cool.

Reduce oven to 375°.

Melt butter in a large skillet over medium heat. Add apples; cook and stir until tender, about 10 minutes. Stir in 3 tablespoons granulated sugar. Cool 15 minutes.

Spread cream filling into prepared crust. Place apples in overlapping circles on top of filling. Bake 15 minutes. Sprinkle with 1 tablespoon granulated sugar; bake until filling is set, about 10 minutes. Cool slightly before serving. Refrigerate leftovers. Makes 8 servings.

APPLE TARTE TATIN

A simple dessert…serve warm.

**6 Golden Delicious apples, peeled, halved and carefully cored
juice of 1 lemon**

**1 cup granulated sugar
¼ cup water
4 tablespoons unsalted butter**

1 sheet 12x17-inch frozen puff pastry, thawed

Preheat oven to 400°.
Place apples in a bowl and sprinkle with lemon juice; drain and set aside.

Stir and cook sugar and water in a heavy oven-proof skillet, about 7 minutes. Add butter; stir to melt. Place as many apples as you can fit in skillet, round side down. Remove from heat.

Roll out pastry on a lightly floured surface into a 14-inch circle about ⅛-inch thick. Place over apples in skillet. Fold edges under and crimp. Make 3 small slits on top to vent steam. Bake 10 minutes, then reduce heat to 375° and continue baking about 25 minutes. Pastry will be golden brown.

Cool 2 minutes, then loosen edges with a knife. Place a serving plate over skillet and carefully invert. Refrigerate leftovers.

Makes 8 servings.

MINNESOTA APPLE CREAM CHEESE TART

Honeycrisp or Golden Delicious apples are a good choice for this cream cheese tart.

Crust
1 cup all-purpose flour
½ cup butter, softened
⅓ cup granulated sugar
¼ teaspoon pure vanilla extract

Filling
2 8-ounce packages cream cheese, softened
½ cup granulated sugar
2 eggs
1 teaspoon pure vanilla extract

Topping
4 cups apples, peeled, cored and sliced ¼-inch thick
⅓ cup granulated sugar
½ teaspoon ground cinnamon
½ teaspoon ground nutmeg
pinch ground cardamom, optional

¼ cup sliced almonds

Preheat oven to 375°.
Crust: Beat all crust ingredients in a small bowl on medium speed until dough leaves sides of bowl and forms a ball. Press dough onto bottom of a 10-inch springform pan.

Filling: Beat all filling ingredients in a bowl on medium speed until smooth. Pour into prepared crust.

Topping: Mix all topping ingredients except almonds in a large bowl. Arrange apples in an overlapping circle pattern over cream cheese layer. Bake 45–55 minutes or until apples are tender. Sprinkle with almonds and continue baking until almonds are light brown, about 5 minutes. Loosen tart from rim of pan with a thin metal spatula. Cool completely in pan, then remove rim. Refrigerate leftovers.

Makes 12 servings.

APPLE TORTE

Top with thawed non-dairy whipped topping when serving.

Crust
½ cup butter
⅓ cup granulated sugar
1 teaspoon grated orange rind
1 cup all-purpose flour

Filling
1 8-ounce package cream cheese, softened
⅓ cup granulated sugar
2 eggs
1 teaspoon fresh lemon juice
1 teaspoon pure vanilla extract
1 teaspoon ground cinnamon
¼ teaspoon ground nutmeg
1 20-ounce can apple pie filling

Preheat oven to 425°.
Crust: Beat butter and sugar until creamy; beat in orange rind. Stir in flour until well blended. Pat dough onto bottom and up sides of a buttered 10-inch springform pan.

Filling: Beat cream cheese and sugar in a medium bowl until creamy. Beat in eggs, lemon juice and vanilla. Stir in cinnamon, nutmeg and pie filling. Spoon into prepared crust. Bake 10 minutes. Reduce heat to 375° and continue baking about 20 minutes or until a knife inserted in center comes out clean. Cool; remove rim. Refrigerate.

Makes 12 servings.

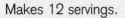

BAVARIAN APPLE TORTE

Top with cinnamon whipped cream when serving.

Crust
½ cup butter or margarine
⅓ cup granulated sugar
¼ teaspoon pure vanilla extract
1 cup all-purpose flour

Filling
1 8-ounce package cream cheese,
 softened
¼ cup granulated sugar
1 egg
½ teaspoon pure vanilla extract

Topping
4 cups peeled, cored and thinly
 sliced Granny Smith apples
⅓ cup granulated sugar
½ teaspoon ground cinnamon
¼ cup sliced almonds

Preheat oven to 450°.
Crust: Beat butter and sugar in a bowl until light and fluffy. Beat in vanilla.
Add flour; mix well. Spread dough onto bottom and 1½ inches up the sides
of a 9-inch springform pan.

Filling: Beat cream cheese and sugar in a medium bowl until blended. Beat
in egg and vanilla. Pour into prepared crust.

Topping: Mix apples, sugar and cinnamon in a bowl until apples are coated.
Spoon over cream cheese layer. Sprinkle with almonds. Bake at 450° for
10 minutes. Reduce heat to 400° and continue baking 25 minutes. Run a
thin knife around side of pan to loosen. Cool; remove side of pan.
Refrigerate and chill torte well before serving. Refrigerate leftovers.

Makes 8 servings.

APPLESAUCE TORTE

Serve with cinnamon sweetened whipped cream.

24 graham crackers, crushed
8 tablespoons butter, melted

3 pounds, peeled, cored and sliced Jonathan or Baldwin apples
6 eggs yolks, beaten
1 cup sweetened condensed milk
3 tablespoons fresh lemon juice
1 tablespoon grated lemon rind
½ teaspoon pure vanilla extract
6 egg whites, stiffly beaten

Preheat oven to 350°.
Mix graham cracker crumbs and butter in a bowl; spread half the mixture into a greased 9-inch springform baking pan.

Cook apples with a little water in a saucepan over medium heat. Mash to form applesauce. Add egg yolks, sweetened condensed milk, lemon juice, lemon rind and vanilla; mix well. Fold in stiffly beaten egg whites. Pour into crumb-lined pan. Cover with remaining crumbs. Bake until firm and lightly browned, 45–60 minutes. Cool. Refrigerate leftovers.

Makes 10 servings.

GOLDEN DELICIOUS APPLE TORTE

Serve with a dollop of whipped cream.

Crust
2 cups all-purpose flour
½ cup granulated sugar
1 teaspoons baking powder
⅛ teaspoon salt
½ cup soft butter or margarine
1 egg
2 tablespoons cold water

Filling
5 Golden Delicious apples,
  peeled, cored and sliced
2 tablespoons fresh lemon juice
1 teaspoon pure vanilla extract
¼ cup raisins
⅓ cup granulated sugar
2 tablespoons all-purpose flour
1 teaspoon ground cinnamon

Preheat oven to 400°.
Crust: Sift flour, sugar, baking powder and salt into a medium bowl. Blend in butter, egg and water with fingers until a dough forms. Reserve one-third of the dough. Pat remaining dough on bottom and halfway up the sides of a greased 9-inch springform pan. Bake 10 minutes; set aside.

Reduce heat to 350°.
Filling: Mix apples, lemon juice, vanilla and raisins in a bowl, then sprinkle with sugar, flour and cinnamon; mix well. Spoon into prepared crust. Roll out reserved dough into ½-inch-wide strips; place over apples, forming a lattice pattern; crimp to edge of baked crust. Return to oven, and continue baking 50–60 minutes or until apples are tender and crust is golden brown. Refrigerate leftovers.

Makes 10 servings.

LINZER APPLE TORTE

Serve plain or with whipped cream.

Crust
1½ cups all-purpose flour
1 cup ground hazelnuts or almonds
⅓ cup granulated sugar
¼ teaspoon ground cinnamon
½ cup butter
1 egg, beaten

Filling
¼ cup butter
6 cups peeled, cored and sliced apples
1 tablespoon fresh lemon juice
1 teaspoon pure vanilla extract
⅓ cup granulated sugar
2 tablespoons all-purpose flour
⅛ teaspoon ground nutmeg
½ cup red raspberry preserves, melted

Preheat oven to 375°.
Crust: Mix flour, hazelnuts, sugar and cinnamon in a medium bowl. Cut in butter with a pastry blender until mixtures resembles small peas. Stir in egg until well blended. Form mixture into dough. Reserve one-quarter of the dough. Pat remaining dough onto bottom and 1¼ inches up the sides of a lightly buttered 9-inch springform pan.

Filling: Melt butter in a large saucepan. Add apples and lemon juice; cook and stir until apples are just tender. Remove from heat. Stir in vanilla. Mix sugar, flour and nutmeg in a small bowl; stir into apple mixture. Spoon into prepared crust. Bake 35–40 minutes or until crust is brown and apples are tender. Cool on a rack. Remove rim.

Roll out reserved dough to ⅛-inch thickness; cut out 10 star shapes or other shapes; place on a baking sheet. Bake at 375° until lightly browned. Cool. When serving, spread melted preserves on top of torte and top with baked stars. Refrigerate leftovers.

Makes 10 servings.

Muffins
Breads

APPLE-CARROT MUFFINS

Serve warm or at room temperature with softened butter.

1½ cups all-purpose flour
1½ cups raisin bran cereal
¾ cup granulated sugar
1¼ teaspoons baking soda
¼ teaspoon salt
¾ teaspoon ground cinnamon

1 large egg, beaten
¾ cup buttermilk
¼ cup corn oil
1 teaspoon pure vanilla extract

¾ cup peeled, cored, finely chopped tart apples
¾ cup grated fresh carrots
¼ cup chopped walnuts or pecans

Preheat oven to 400°.
Grease or paper line muffin pan.

Mix first six ingredients in a large bowl until well blended.

Stir egg, buttermilk, corn oil and vanilla in a small bowl; stir into first mixture until just moistened. Stir in apples, carrots and walnuts. Spoon batter into prepared pan. Bake 20–25 minutes or until a wooden pick inserted in center comes out clean. Cool on a rack 5 minutes. Remove from pan. Serve or cool on a wire rack.

Makes 12 muffins.

APPLE CHEDDAR MUFFINS

Muffins baked in paper liners makes clean-up easy.

1 egg, lightly beaten
½ cup whole milk
¼ cup corn oil
1 cup applesauce
¼ cup granulated sugar

1½ cups all-purpose flour
2 teaspoons baking powder
½ teaspoon salt
½ teaspoon ground cinnamon
½ cup shredded sharp cheddar cheese

Preheat oven to 400°.
Grease or paper line muffin pan.

Mix egg, milk, corn oil, applesauce and sugar in a large bowl.

Mix flour, baking powder, salt and cinnamon in a small bowl until blended. Stir flour mixture and cheese into wet mixture just until flour is moistened. Spoon batter equally into prepared muffin pan. Bake 20–25 minutes. Cool in pan 5 minutes. If necessary, run a thin knife around edges of muffins to loosen, then remove from pan and cool on a wire rack. Serve or store in refrigerator.

Makes 12 muffins.

APPLE-CRANBERRY MUFFINS

Apples and cranberries…a good combination.

1¾ cups all-purpose flour
¼ cup granulated sugar
1½ teaspoons baking powder
½ teaspoon baking soda
½ teaspoon salt

1 egg
¾ cup whole milk
¾ cup sweetened applesauce
¼ cup butter or margarine, melted and slightly cooled
½ teaspoon pure vanilla extract
1 cup fresh cranberries, coarsely chopped, tossed with
   2 tablespoons all-purpose flour

¼ cup granulated sugar mixed with ½ teaspoon ground cinnamon

Preheat oven to 400°.
Grease or paper line muffin pan.

Mix first five ingredients in a large bowl until blended.

In another bowl, whisk egg, milk, applesauce, butter and vanilla; stir into first mixture until moistened. Stir in cranberry mixture. Spoon batter into prepared pan. Sprinkle with sugar-cinnamon mixture. Bake 20–25 minutes or until a wooden pick inserted in center comes out clean. Remove from pan. Serve or cool completely on a rack.

Makes 12 muffins.

APPLE STREUSEL MUFFINS

Serve these warm streusel muffins for a delicious coffee break.

2 cups all-purpose flour
¼ cup granulated sugar
¼ cup brown sugar
½ teaspoon ground cinnamon
2 teaspoons baking powder
½ teaspoon baking soda
½ teaspoon salt

Streusel
2 tablespoons all-purpose flour
1 tablespoon brown sugar, packed
¼ teaspoon ground cinnamon
1 tablespoon butter, cut up

1 cup buttermilk
¼ cup corn oil
1 egg
1 teaspoon pure vanilla extract
1 large apple, peeled, cored and coarsely chopped

Preheat oven to 400°.
Grease or paper line muffin pan.

Streusel: Mix all streusel ingredients until crumbly.

Mix first seven ingredients in a large bowl until blended.

In another bowl, whisk buttermilk, corn oil, egg and vanilla; stir into first mixture until moistened. Stir in apple. Spoon batter into prepared pan. Sprinkle with streusel. Bake 20–25 minutes or until a wooden pick inserted in center comes out clean. Cool on a rack 5 minutes, then remove from pan. Serve warm or cool completely on a rack.

Makes 12 muffins.

APPLESAUCE BRAN MUFFINS

Applesauce and bran make a delicious way to start breakfast.

1¼ cups bran cereal (not flakes)
⅔ cup whole milk
⅔ cup applesauce
½ teaspoon pure vanilla extract
¼ cup granulated sugar
1 tablespoon baking powder
¾ teaspoon salt

1 egg
¼ cup butter or margarine, melted and cooled slightly
1 cup all-purpose flour

Preheat oven to 400°.
Grease or paper line muffin pan.

Place bran in a large mixing bowl. Add milk and soak 10 minutes. Stir in applesauce, vanilla, sugar, baking powder and salt.

Whisk egg and butter in a small bowl; stir into bran mixture until blended. Stir in flour until moistened. Spoon batter into prepared pan. Bake 20–30 minutes or until a wooden pick inserted in center comes out clean. Cool on a rack 5 minutes, then remove from pan and cool completely on a rack.

Makes 12 muffins.

RHUBARB APPLESAUCE MUFFINS

Serve these giant muffins warm with softened butter.

2 cups all-purpose flour
1 cup whole wheat flour
2 teaspoons baking powder
½ teaspoon baking soda
½ teaspoon salt
2 teaspoons ground cinnamon

2 eggs
1⅛ cup brown sugar, packed
½ cup corn oil
1⅛ cups applesauce
1 teaspoon pure vanilla extract
1½ cup chopped rhubarb

Preheat oven to 350°.
Grease or paper line muffin pan with 3½-inch cups.

Mix first six ingredients in a large bowl until well blended.

Beat eggs, brown sugar and corn oil in a medium bowl; stir in applesauce and vanilla. Stir into flour mixture just until flour is moistened. Fold in rhubarb. Spoon batter into prepared muffin cups, filling each two-thirds full. Bake 30–35 minutes or until tops are firm and golden. Remove from pans to a wire rack.

Makes 10 giant muffins.

129

SAM'S APPLE MUFFINS

Apple, walnut, cinnamon muffins…like Sam, unforgettable.

2 cups all-purpose flour
½ cup granulated sugar
1½ teaspoons baking powder
½ teaspoon baking soda
½ teaspoon salt
1 teaspoon ground cinnamon
⅛ teaspoon ground nutmeg

¾ cup whole milk
1 large egg
¼ cup butter, melted and slightly cooled
1 teaspoon pure vanilla extract

½ cup coarsely chopped walnuts
2 tart green apples, peeled, cored and coarsely chopped,
   tossed with 2 tablespoons fresh lemon juice.

Preheat oven to 400°.
Grease or paper line muffin pan.

Mix first seven ingredients in a large bowl until blended.

In another bowl, whisk milk, egg, butter and vanilla; stir into first mixture
until moistened. Stir in walnuts and apples. Spoon into prepared pan. Bake
20–25 minutes or until a wooden pick inserted comes out clean. Cool on a
wire rack 5 minutes, then remove from pan. Serve warm or cool completely
on a rack.

Makes 12 muffins.

APPLE BUTTER BREAD

Apple butter was always a treat spread on plain white bread...now try this good bread spread with softened butter.

2 cups all-purpose flour
1 cup brown sugar, packed
1½ teaspoons baking powder
½ teaspoon baking soda
½ teaspoon salt

1½ cups apple butter, divided
½ cup apple juice
¼ cup butter, melted
1 egg, beaten
1 cup raisins
½ cup chopped walnuts

Preheat oven to 350°.
Grease and flour bottom and sides of a 9x5-inch loaf pan.

In a large bowl, mix first five ingredients.

Stir in ¾ cup apple butter, apple juice, butter and egg. Fold in raisins and walnuts. Spoon half the batter into prepared pan. Spoon remaining ¾ cup apple butter over batter. Gently spread remaining batter over apple butter.

Bake 65–75 minutes or until top springs back when lightly touched in the center. Cool in pan on a wire rack 45 minutes. Remove from pan; cool completely on a wire rack. Wrap in plastic food wrap and refrigerate.

Makes 18 servings.

APPLE CORN BREAD

Serve hot with softened butter.

1 cup yellow cornmeal
1 cup all-purpose flour
¼ cup granulated sugar
1 teaspoon baking soda
1 teaspoon baking powder
¾ teaspoon salt

1 egg
1 cup buttermilk
¼ cup corn oil
1 cup tart apple, peeled, cored and coarsely chopped

Preheat oven to 375°.
Grease an 8x8-inch square baking pan.

Mix first six ingredients in a large bowl until blended.

In another bowl, beat egg; whisk in buttermilk and corn oil. Stir into dry mixture until completely moistened. Stir in apples. Spoon into prepared pan. Bake 35–40 minutes or until a wooden pick inserted in center comes out clean. Cool slightly in pan before cutting into squares.

Makes 8 servings.

APPLE QUICK BREAD

Spread with softened butter or cream cheese when serving.

½ cup butter
1 cup granulated sugar
2 eggs
1 teaspoon pure vanilla extract
2 cups peeled, grated tart apples

2 cups all-purpose flour
1 teaspoon salt
1 teaspoon baking soda
1 teaspoon baking powder
1 teaspoon ground cinnamon
½ teaspoon ground cloves

⅔ cup chopped walnuts
1 tablespoon freshly grated lemon peel

Preheat oven to 350°.
Beat butter and sugar in a bowl until creamy. Beat in eggs, one at a time.
Stir in vanilla and apples.

Sift together dry ingredients in another bowl; stir into creamed mixture until
blended. Stir in walnuts and lemon peel. Pour batter into a greased 9x5-inch
loaf pan. Bake 50 minutes or until a wooden pick inserted in center comes
out clean. Cool in pan 15 minutes. Remove from pan; cool completely on a
wire rack. Wrap in plastic food wrap and store in refrigerator.

Makes 1 loaf.

APPLE STRUDEL MACHINE BREAD

Made easy with the bread machine.

¾ cup milk
⅓ cup margarine or butter,
  cut up
1 egg
3¼ cups bread flour
⅓ cup granulated sugar
¾ teaspoon salt
1 teaspoon active dry yeast
  or bread machine yeast

3 tablespoons margarine or
  butter, softened

3 cups thinly sliced, cored and peeled
  apples
½ cup brown sugar, packed
½ cup raisins
½ teaspoon pure vanilla extract
4 teaspoons all-purpose flour
1 teaspoon ground cinnamon

1 cup powdered sugar
1 tablespoon melted butter
½ teaspoon pure vanilla extract
2 teaspoons fresh orange juice

Line a 15x10x1-inch baking pan with cooking foil; set aside.

Add first seven ingredients to a 1½- or 2-pound bread machine according to the manufacturer's directions. Select the dough cycle. Remove dough from machine when cycle is complete. Punch dough down, and cover with a clean tea towel 10 minutes.

Preheat oven to 350°.

Roll dough out on a lightly floured surface into a 24x12-inch rectangle; brush with softened margarine. Mix apples, brown sugar, raisins, ½ teaspoon vanilla , all-purpose flour and cinnamon in a medium bowl. Starting 2 inches from a long side of dough, spoon apple mixture in a 3-inch-wide strip across dough. Starting from the long side, carefully roll the dough up. Brush edge with a little water; seal seam and ends. Carefully place roll, seam down, in the prepared pan. Curve the roll to form a crescent shape. Cover and let rise in a warm place until nearly doubled, about 45 minutes. Bake 30–35 minutes or until golden brown. Cool completely in pan on a wire rack.

Beat powdered sugar, melted butter, ½ teaspoon vanilla and just enough orange juice in a small bowl to a drizzle consistency. Drizzle over bread. Makes 1 loaf.

APPLE WHOLE WHEAT BREAD

Serve this wholesome apple bread anytime.

¾ cup warm water (not hot)
2 tablespoons granulated sugar
1 package dry yeast
1 cup bran cereal (not flakes)

1 cup whole milk
2 tablespoons butter or margarine
¾ teaspoon salt

2 cups whole wheat flour
2 medium apples, peeled,
   cored and coarsely chopped
½ cup dark raisins
1½–2 cups bread flour

Stir water, sugar and yeast in a large mixing bowl until yeast is dissolved. Blend in bran; set aside to soften.

In a saucepan, stir milk, butter and salt over medium heat until butter is melted. Remove from heat; cool until milk is barely warm to touch, then stir into the softened bran mixture. Stir in whole wheat flour, apples and raisins. Stir in enough bread flour to form a dough stiff enough to knead; knead dough on a floured surface, working in as much bread flour until dough is soft and no longer sticks to work surface. Place in a greased bowl. Cover with a clean kitchen towel and let rise until doubled.

Preheat oven to 375°. Grease a 9x5-inch loaf pan. Punch down dough, then place on floured surface and shape into a loaf. Place into prepared pan. Cover loosely with a clean kitchen towel, and let rise until doubled. Bake 35–45 minutes or until loaf sounds hollow when tapped on top. Place on a wire rack; cool in pan 5 minutes, then remove from pan and cool completely on wire rack.

Makes 1 loaf.

APPLESAUCE RAISIN BREAD

A slice of this moist applesauce bread is always a welcomed treat.

2 cups all-purpose flour
2 teaspoons baking powder
½ teaspoon baking soda
½ teaspoon salt
¾ teaspoon ground cinnamon
¼ teaspoon ground nutmeg
⅛ teaspoon ground cloves

½ cup solid vegetable shortening
1 cup granulated sugar
2 large eggs
1 teaspoon pure vanilla extract
1 cup unsweetened applesauce
1 cup dark raisins
½ cup coarsely chopped walnuts

Preheat oven to 350°.
Generously grease a 9x5-inch loaf pan.

Mix first seven ingredients in a large bowl until blended.

Beat shortening and sugar in a bowl on high speed until light and fluffy.
Beat in eggs and vanilla.

Beat in dry mixture on low speed, alternating with applesauce until well
moistened. Stir in raisins and walnuts by hand.

Spoon batter into prepared pan. Bake 50–60 minutes or until a wooden
pick inserted in center comes out clean. Cover top with cooking foil last 10
minutes of baking to prevent browning too fast. Cool in pan 10 minutes;
remove from pan; cool on a wire rack.

Makes 1 loaf.

CHOCOLATE APPLESAUCE BREAD

For garnish, mix 1 teaspoon cocoa powder with 1 teaspoon powdered sugar and sprinkle on top of cooled bread.

½ cup butter, softened
1⅓ cups granulated sugar
2 eggs
1½ cups unsweetened applesauce
1 teaspoon pure vanilla extract

3 cups all-purpose flour
¼ cup unsweetened cocoa powder
1¾ teaspoons baking soda
½ teaspoon salt
½ teaspoon ground cinnamon
⅛ teaspoon nutmeg
⅔ cup milk chocolate chips
½ cup dry-roasted unsalted peanuts, chopped

Preheat oven to 350°.
Generously grease two 8½x4½-inch loaf pans.

Beat butter and sugar on low speed until fluffy, about 2 minutes. Beat in eggs one at a time. Beat in applesauce and vanilla on low speed.

In another bowl, mix flour, cocoa powder, soda, salt, cinnamon and nutmeg until blended. Add to first mixture on low speed until moistened. Stir in chocolate chips and peanuts by hand. Spoon into prepared pans. Bake 60–70 minutes or until a wooden pick inserted in center comes out clean. Cool in pan 15 minutes. Remove from pan; cool completely on a wire rack.

Makes 2 loaves.

FRESH LEMON POPPYSEED APPLESAUCE LOAF

Lemon and poppyseeds paired with applesauce.

2½ cups all-purpose flour
2 teaspoons baking powder
½ teaspoon baking soda
½ teaspoon salt
¼ cup poppyseeds
1 cup granulated sugar
⅔ cup natural applesauce
1 large egg

2 egg whites, lightly beaten
2 tablespoons corn oil
1 tablespoon grated fresh lemon peel
1 teaspoon pure vanilla extract
⅓ cup whole milk

Lemon syrup
¼ cup granulated sugar
¼ cup fresh lemon juice

Preheat oven to 350°.
Grease a 9x5-inch loaf pan.

In a large bowl, mix flour, baking powder, soda, salt and poppyseeds.

In a medium bowl, mix sugar, applesauce, egg, egg whites, corn oil, lemon peel and vanilla. Stir into first mixture alternately with milk until completely moistened. Spoon batter into prepared pan.

Bake about 40–45 minutes or until a wooden pick inserted in center comes out clean. Cool in pan 10 minutes. Remove from pan; cool on a wire rack. Pierce top of loaf with metal skewer.

Lemon syrup: In a small saucepan, stir sugar and lemon juice until sugar is dissolved. Cool slightly. Brush lemon syrup over loaf. Cool before slicing. Refrigerate leftovers.

Makes 16 servings.

Scones
Biscuits
Popovers
Fritters
Doughnuts
Turnovers

APPLE CHEDDAR SCONES

Serve warm with soft butter and apple jelly.

1½ cups all-purpose flour
½ cup toasted wheat germ
3 tablespoons granulated sugar
2 teaspoons baking powder
½ teaspoon salt

3 tablespoons butter
1 Golden Delicious apple, cored and finely chopped
¼ cup shredded cheddar cheese

1 egg
½ cup milk

Preheat oven to 400°.
Grease an 8-inch round cake pan.

Mix first five ingredients in a medium bowl until blended. Cut in butter with a pastry blender until crumbly. Stir in apple and cheese.

Beat egg and milk in a small bowl; add to flour mixture. Stir until a soft dough is formed. Knead dough on a lightly floured surface until smooth. Spread dough evenly into prepared pan. Score deeply with a knife to make 6 wedges but do not cut all the way through. Bake 25–30 minutes or until top springs back with lightly pressed. Remove from pan to a rack.

Makes 6 servings.

APPLE-CRANBERRY SCONES

Serve warm.

2 cups all-purpose flour
1 cup quick-cooking oatmeal
⅓ cup granulated sugar
2 teaspoons baking powder
½ teaspoon salt
½ teaspoon baking soda
½ teaspoon ground cinnamon

½ cup unsweetened applesauce, divided
2 tablespoons margarine
½ cup coarsely chopped cranberries
½ cup peeled, chopped apple

¼ cup whole milk
6 tablespoons honey, divided
1 teaspoon pure vanilla extract

Preheat oven to 425°.
Spray baking sheet with nonstick cooking spray.

Mix first seven ingredients in a large bowl until blended.

Add ¼ cup applesauce and margarine; cut into first mixture with pastry blender until crumbly. Stir in cranberries and apple.

Whisk milk, ¼ cup honey and vanilla in a small bowl; add to flour mixture and stir until dough forms a ball. Knead dough until smooth on a well-floured surface, then form into an 8-inch circle. Place on prepared baking sheet. Score dough into 12 wedges; do not cut all the way through.

Mix ¼ cup applesauce and 2 tablespoons honey in a cup; brush over top of dough. Bake 12–15 minutes or until lightly browned. Remove from baking sheet immediately; cool on a wire rack 10 minutes. Cut into wedges. Serve or cool on a rack.

Makes 12 servings.

APPLESAUCE BISCUITS

A nice treat for that mid-morning coffee break.

1½ cups all-purpose flour
½ cup whole wheat flour
2 tablespoons brown sugar
1½ teaspoons baking powder
½ teaspoon baking soda
½ teaspoon salt
½ teaspoon ground cinnamon
¼ teaspoon ground allspice

¼ cup solid shortening

⅔ cup applesauce
2 tablespoons whole milk

Preheat oven to 425°.
Lightly grease a baking sheet.

Whisk the first eight ingredients in a large bowl until well blended. Cut in shortening until crumbly.

Mix applesauce and milk in a small bowl; stir into flour mixture with a fork and form into a ball. Knead dough on a lightly floured surface until smooth, sifting in flour if necessary to prevent sticking. Pat dough into a circle, then roll out to ¾-inch thickness. Cut out with a 2-inch biscuit cutter; place on prepared baking sheet. Bake 12–15 minutes or until lightly browned. Serve immediately or cool on a rack.

Makes 15 biscuits.

APPLE POPOVERS

These popovers are similar to a fluffy apple pancake.

2 eggs
1 cup whole milk
1 cup all-purpose flour
¼ teaspoon salt
1 tablespoon granulated sugar
2 tablespoons melted butter

6 tablespoons cold butter
1 Granny Smith apple, peeled, cored and cut into ½-inch cubes
1 cup raisins

Preheat oven to 425°.
Whisk eggs and milk in a medium bowl. Add flour, salt and sugar; whisk until blended. Whisk in melted butter.

Place equal amounts of cold butter into the unlined cups of a regular 12-muffin pan. Spoon an equal amount of apple and raisins into each cup. Place the muffin pan in the oven for 5 minutes, until butter is melted and apples slightly cooked.

Remove muffin pan from oven, and immediately pour batter into each cup, filling each halfway. Bake for 10 minutes at 425°, then reduce heat to 375° and bake until popovers are puffed and golden brown, about 15–20 minutes. Serve hot.

Makes 1 dozen.

APPLE FRITTERS

Serve hot. Sprinkle with powdered sugar if desired.

1¾ cups all-purpose flour
2 tablespoons granulated sugar
2 teaspoons baking powder
½ teaspoon salt
½ teaspoon ground cinnamon
¼ teaspoon ground nutmeg

¾ cup whole milk
2 eggs, separated
2 tablespoons butter or margarine, melted and slightly cooled
1 cup peeled, cored and coarsely chopped apple
corn oil for deep-frying

Heat oil in a deep fryer or heavy deep saucepan to 370°.

Mix first six ingredients in a large bowl until well blended.

Whisk milk, egg yolks and butter in a small bowl; add to flour mixture and beat until well moistened. Stir in apples.

In another bowl, beat egg whites until stiff; fold into apple mixture.

Drop by rounded tablespoonfuls of dough into hot oil a few at a time; do not crowd. Fry until puffy, about 4 minutes, turning the fritters to brown evenly. Remove with slotted spoon; drain on paper towels.

Makes 16 fritters.

APPLESAUCE DOUGHNUTS

Serve warm or at room temperature.

2 large eggs
¾ cup granulated sugar
¼ cup butter or margarine, melted
1 cup applesauce
¼ cup apple juice
1 teaspoon pure vanilla extract

4 cups all-purpose flour, divided
2 teaspoons baking powder
1 teaspoon baking soda
¾ teaspoon salt
1 teaspoon ground cinnamon
½ teaspoon ground nutmeg

corn oil for deep-frying

Beat eggs and sugar in a bowl with an electric mixer on high speed until slightly thickened. Gradually beat in butter. Beat in applesauce, juice and vanilla on low speed until blended.

Whisk 3½ cups flour, baking powder, baking soda, salt, cinnamon and nutmeg in a large bowl until blended. Gradually add to first mixture on low speed; beat until a moist, stiff dough is formed.

Gently knead dough on a lightly floured surface, adding additional flour as necessary, to form a soft, smooth dough. Cover dough with a clean tea towel 30 minutes. Roll dough out to a ½-inch thickness. Cut dough with a 2½-inch doughnut cutter.

Heat corn oil in a deep fryer to 370°. Fry doughnuts, a few at a time, until golden brown on both sides, about 3–4 minutes. Drain on paper towels.

Makes 2 dozen.

CHEESE APPLE TURNOVERS

Apple and cheese...a good combination.

1 10-ounce can refrigerated pizza crust
4 slices deli-style medium cheddar cheese

1 cup canned apple pie filling
1 teaspoon ground cinnamon, divided
1 egg white, beaten
2 teaspoons granulated sugar

Preheat oven to 400°.
Roll crust on a lightly floured surface to form a 10-inch square. Cut into 4 equal pieces; top each with a slice of cheese.

Mix pie filling with ½ teaspoon ground cinnamon in a small bowl. Spoon ¼ cup apple mixture over each cheese slice. Brush edges of crust with egg white; fold in half, forming a triangle. Press edges with tines of fork to seal. Cut small slits in top of crust to vent steam.

Brush remaining egg white over top of turnovers. Mix sugar and remaining cinnamon in a cup; sprinkle over top of turnovers. Bake 18 minutes or until puffed and golden. Cool on a wire rack 10 minutes before serving.

Makes 4 servings.

Appetizers

BAKED APPLESAUCE SAUSAGE APPETIZER

Use wooden picks to serve.

2 pounds Italian sausage
¾ cup brown sugar, packed
1 cup chunky applesauce
1 medium onion, chopped

Preheat oven to 325°.
In a large skillet, cook sausage until browned. Remove from skillet and cut into bite-size pieces. Place into a small baking casserole. Add remaining ingredients; mix well. Bake 45 minutes. Serve warm.

Makes 8 servings.

CRANBERRY-APPLE BAKED BRIE

Serve with crackers and thinly sliced apples.

2 tablespoons maple syrup
1 tablespoon butter, melted
1 small Gala apple, cored, peeled and
    cut into ½-inch pieces, divided
⅓ cup sliced natural almonds, divided
⅓ cup sweetened dried cranberries, divided
1 round whole Brie cheese, about 1 pound

Preheat oven to 350°.
Coat a baking sheet with nonstick vegetable-oil cooking spray.

In a cup, mix maple syrup and butter until well blended. Set aside ⅓ cup apples and 2 tablespoons almonds. Mix remaining apple, remaining almonds, ¼ cup cranberries and 1½ tablespoons maple syrup mixture in a medium bowl.

Split cheese in half horizontally. Place one half, cut side up, on prepared baking sheet. Top with cranberry-apple mixture. Place other half of cheese, cut side down, on top. Brush top with part of the remaining maple syrup mixture. Sprinkle with remaining almonds and cranberries. Top with reserved apples in center. Drizzle remaining maple syrup over all.

Bake 7 minutes or until cheese just begins to melt. Serve immediately.

Makes 16 servings.

MR. BROWN'S COUNTRY RIBS

Appetizers for when the boys get together…putting on the dog!

2 pounds country-style pork ribs, trimmed

1 tablespoon prepared mustard
1 tablespoon cornstarch
1 cup apple juice
¼ cup apple cider vinegar
1 tablespoon Worcestershire sauce
⅛ teaspoon ground black pepper

Preheat oven to 350°.
Place ribs on a rack in a shallow roasting pan. Bake, uncovered, 1 hour.

Blend mustard and cornstarch in a microwave-safe bowl, then whisk in remaining ingredients. Microwave on high for 1 minute. Stir well. Microwave on high for another 4 minutes, stirring twice during cooking period.

Spoon one-third of the mustard mixture over ribs and bake for 30 minutes. Spoon remaining mixture over ribs and bake another 30 minutes. Turn ribs over and spoon mixture from pan over ribs. Bake about 15 minutes or until ribs are no longer pink. Serve hot. Refrigerate leftovers.

Makes 6 servings.

Salads
Soups

APPLESAUCE RASPBERRY GELATIN SALAD

Add finely chopped nuts, for variation, if desired.

1 cup dairy sour cream
2 cups miniature marshmallows

1 6-ounce package raspberry-flavored gelatin
2 tablespoons granulated sugar
2¾ cups boiling water
1 10-ounce package frozen raspberries in syrup
2 cups applesauce

Mix sour cream and marshmallows in a glass bowl. Cover and refrigerate until marshmallows are softened.

Stir gelatin and sugar in boiling water in a bowl until gelatin is dissolved. Add frozen raspberries; stir until thawed. Stir in applesauce. Pour mixture into a 13x9x2-inch glass baking dish. Refrigerate until set.

Remove sour cream mixture from refrigerator; beat with an electric mixer until smooth. Spoon over firm gelatin; spread evenly. Refrigerate leftovers.

Makes 10 servings.

CHERRY-APPLE CREAM CHEESE GELATIN MOLD

For variation, use a different gelatin flavor such as cranberry.

1½ cups boiling water
1 package 8-serving size cherry-flavored gelatin
2 cups cold apple juice
1 unpeeled Red Delicious apple, cored and thinly sliced

1 8-ounce package cream cheese, softened

Stir boiling water and gelatin in a large bowl until completely dissolved. Stir in apple juice. Set aside 1 cup gelatin mixture at room temperature. Refrigerate remaining gelatin until thickened, about 1½ hours. Spoon half of the thickened gelatin into a 6-cup mold sprayed with cooking spray; top with a single layer of apple slices, slightly overlapping. Cover with remaining thickened gelatin. Refrigerate 30 minutes or until set but not firm.

Beat cream cheese in a medium bowl until creamy. Gradually beat in reserved gelatin until well blended. Pour over gelatin layer in mold. Refrigerate until firm, about 4 hours. Unmold on a serving platter. Refrigerate leftovers.

Makes 10 servings.

CRANBERRY APPLESAUCE GELATIN SALAD

A good salad for Thanksgiving dinner.

2 4-serving size packages strawberry-flavored gelatin
1½ cups boiling water
½ cup salad dressing
1 12-ounce container cranberry-orange sauce
1½ cups sweetened applesauce

Stir gelatin and boiling water in a bowl until completely dissolved. Gradually stir in salad dressing until smooth. Stir in cranberry-orange sauce and applesauce. Pour mixture into a 5-cup ring mold coated with cooking spray. Refrigerate until firm. Unmold onto a serving plate. Refrigerate leftovers.

Makes 8 servings.

AVOCADO-APPLE CHICKEN SALAD

Serve over a bed of lettuce, along with warm rolls and soft butter.

1 pound boneless, skinless chicken breasts

¼ cup mayonnaise
3 tablespoons whole milk
2 tablespoons green pepper sauce, such as Tabasco
2 tablespoons fresh lime juice
¾ teaspoon salt

3 stalks celery, sliced
1 green bell pepper, chopped
1 small avocado, sliced
1 Granny Smith apple, cored and cut into ½-inch chunks
1 cup seedless grapes

Place chicken in a 10-inch saucepan with enough water to cover. Bring to a boil over high heat. Reduce heat to low; cover and simmer about 15 minutes or until chicken is cooked through. Drain; cool completely. Cut into ½-inch chunks.

Mix mayonnaise, milk, pepper sauce, lime juice and salt in a small bowl until blended.

Mix cooled chicken, celery, green bell pepper, avocado, apple and grapes in a large bowl. Add mayonnaise mixture and stir until well combined. Refrigerate leftovers.

Makes 4 servings.

CALIFORNIA APPLE-VEGGIE SALAD

Serve with warm French bread and soft butter.

Dressing
¼ cup apple cider vinegar
⅓ cup vegetable oil
1 teaspoon Worcestershire sauce
1 clove garlic, minced
¼ teaspoon dried oregano leaves
½ teaspoon granulated sugar
pinch ground black pepper

Salad
1 cup unpeeled, cored and diced Granny Smith apples
1 cup unpeeled, cored and diced Gala apples
¼ cup sliced fresh mushrooms, optional
¼ cup sliced green onions, including tops
1½ cups torn Bibb or butter lettuce
1½ cups torn fresh spinach
6 slices bacon, cooked crisp and crumbled
¼ cup crumbled feta or blue cheese

Mix all dressing ingredients in a jar. Shake well and refrigerate several hours.

Toss all salad ingredients, except cheese, in a large bowl until well mixed. Serve on individual plates. Sprinkle each serving with cheese and drizzle with dressing as desired. Refrigerate leftovers.

Makes 4 servings.

CHICKEN WALDORF SALAD

Serve with warm hard rolls...buttered, of course.

⅔ cup light mayonnaise
2 tablespoons fresh lemon juice

2 cups cut-up cooked chicken
2 medium apples, unpeeled, cored and chopped
⅔ cup thinly sliced celery
½ cup chopped walnuts, toasted
salt and ground black pepper to taste

Mix mayonnaise and lemon juice in a large glass bowl.

Add remaining ingredients; toss until well mixed. Serve on a bed of lettuce or chill slightly before serving. Refrigerate leftovers.

Makes 4 servings.

CHICKEN APPLE SALAD

Add ½ cup green seedless grapes for variation.

2 Fuji apples, cored and diced
2 cups diced, fully cooked, boneless, skinless chicken breast
¼ cup chopped green pepper
2 teaspoons chopped pimiento
¼ cup mayonnaise
pinch crushed rosemary
pinch lemon pepper
pinch salt

shredded lettuce
alfalfa sprouts

Mix all ingredients except lettuce and alfalfa sprouts in a bowl. Serve on a bed of lettuce; top with alfalfa sprouts. Refrigerate leftovers.

Makes 4 servings.

GRILLED CHICKEN APPLE SALAD

Serve this good salad with warm hard rolls and butter.

2 cups fresh white bread cubes
¼ cup Italian salad dressing

1 10-ounce package mixed salad greens
8 ounces fully cooked grilled chicken breast, cut into strips
1 Golden Delicious apple, cored and chopped
1 cup chopped fresh pineapple
¼ cup Italian dressing

½ cup crumbled feta cheese

Preheat oven to 375°.
Mix bread cubes with dressing. Place bread cubes on a cookie sheet in single layers. Bake until lightly browned, about 8 minutes. Remove from cookie sheet; cool completely.

Mix salad greens, chicken, apple and pineapple in a large bowl. Add salad dressing and toasted bread cubes. Toss to coat. Sprinkle with cheese. Refrigerate leftovers.

Makes 4 servings.

WALDORF TURKEY SALAD

Serve on a bed of lettuce, along with warm hard rolls or bread sticks.

½ cup mayonnaise
2 tablespoons honey
1 cup sliced celery
¼ cup coarsely chopped walnuts
½ pound ½-inch sliced deli turkey breast, cut into ½-inch dice
¼ pound ½-inch thick deli Swiss cheese, cut into ½-inch dice
2 cups unpeeled Red Delicious apples, cored and coarsely
  chopped

Mix mayonnaise and honey in a large bowl until blended. Stir in remaining ingredients until coated. Serve or refrigerate.

Makes 6 servings.

APPLE-CRANBERRY SALAD WITH SOUR CREAM DRESSING

Quick and tasty salad.

Dressing
⅔ cup dairy sour cream
⅓ cup mayonnaise

Salad
2 cups Red Delicious apples, unpeeled, cored and
cut into ½-inch cubes
2 teaspoons fresh lemon juice
½ cup sweetened dried cranberries
½ cup seedless green grapes, halved
½ cup chopped walnuts
½ cup chopped celery

Dressing: Mix sour cream and mayonnaise in a small bowl; set aside.

Salad: Toss apples and lemon juice in a large bowl. Add remaining salad ingredients. Add dressing; toss to coat well. Cover and chill 1 hour before serving. Refrigerate leftovers.

Makes 8 servings.

APPLE POPPYSEED SLAW

This is a good salad to serve with pork or chicken.

8 cups shredded green cabbage
2½ cups peeled and coarsely grated carrots
3 medium Granny Smith apples, peeled, cored and coarsely grated
4 green onions, thinly sliced
2 tablespoons apple cider vinegar

⅔ cup dairy sour cream
½ cup mayonnaise
¼ cup frozen apple juice concentrate, thawed
2 tablespoons poppyseeds
salt and black pepper to taste

Mix first five ingredients in a large bowl.

Whisk remaining ingredients in a medium bowl; add to cabbage mixture and toss until blended. Cover and refrigerate at least one hour before serving. Refrigerate leftovers.

Makes 8 servings.

APPLE-SPINACH SALAD

Apples and spinach topped with a blue cheese dressing.

Dressing
⅔ **cup plain yogurt**
2 **tablespoons mayonnaise**
2 **tablespoons crumbled blue cheese**
⅛ **teaspoon ground black pepper**

Salad
8 **unpeeled Red Delicious apples, cored, cut into ¼-inch slices**
1 **tablespoon fresh lemon juice**
4 **cups packed spinach leaves**
2 **cups thinly sliced celery**
¼ **cup chopped walnuts, toasted**

croutons

Dressing: Mix all dressing ingredients in a small bowl. Cover and chill.

Place apples in a large glass bowl; sprinkle with lemon juice. Add spinach, celery and walnuts; toss. Add chilled salad dressing; toss gently. Serve topped with toasted croutons. Refrigerate leftovers.

Makes 8 servings.

APPLE SALAD WITH BOILED DRESSING

A special apple salad.

Dressing
2 8-ounce cans pineapple chunks, cut in half
½ cup granulated sugar
2 tablespoons all-purpose flour
2 eggs, well beaten
1 tablespoon butter
½ teaspoon pure vanilla extract
½ cup whipping cream, whipped

Salad
6 medium size apples, cored and diced
2 tablespoon fresh lemon juice
1 cup miniature marshmallows
½ cup chopped walnuts
½ cup seedless grapes

Dressing: Drain pineapple, reserving ⅔ cup juice. Cut pineapple chunks in half. Mix sugar and flour in a heavy saucepan. Stir in eggs and reserved pineapple juice. Bring to a boil; boil and stir 1 minute or until mixture is thickened. Remove from heat; stir in butter and vanilla. Refrigerate until cold. Fold in whipped cream.

Salad: Toss apples and lemon juice in a large bowl. Add marshmallows, walnuts and grapes. Fold in ⅓ cup dressing. When serving, pass around remaining dressing. Refrigerate leftovers.

Makes 8 servings.

CRAN-APPLE SALAD

Good with turkey or ham.

2 16-ounce cans whole berry cranberry sauce
2 medium size Granny Smith apples, unpeeled, cored and diced
½ cup thinly sliced celery
1 cup chopped walnuts

Mix all ingredients except walnuts in a glass bowl. Cover and refrigerate until chilled. Stir in walnuts. Serve. Refrigerate leftovers.

Makes 8 servings.

DATE-APPLE-PINEAPPLE SALAD

This is a tasty salad to serve with turkey or ham sandwiches.

2 cups peeled, cored and coarsely chopped apples
½ cup cut-up dates
1 8-ounce can pineapple chunks, drained
1 stalk chopped celery
¼ cup chopped pecans
½ cup miniature marshmallows
½ cup salad dressing or mayonnaise

Mix all ingredients in a glass bowl. Store in refrigerator.

Makes 4 servings.

LOUISIANA SWEET POTATO APPLE SALAD

Louisiana is famous for sweet potatoes…and other good things!

4 cups baked sweet potatoes, peeled and cubed
1 20-ounce can pineapple chunks, drained
4 cups miniature marshmallows
4 Golden Delicious apples, peeled, cored and chopped
½ cup flaked coconut
½ cup chopped walnuts or pecans

1 10-ounce container frozen non-dairy topping, thawed
¾ cup mayonnaise or salad dressing

Mix first six ingredients in a large glass bowl.

Mix topping and mayonnaise in a bowl; fold into apple mixture. Cover and chill well before serving. Refrigerate leftovers.

Makes 10 servings.

ORANGE-CRANBERRY-APPLE SALAD

Good salad to serve along with cold turkey sandwiches.

2 seedless oranges, peeled and coarsely chopped
2 16-ounce cans whole berry cranberry sauce
2 cups coarsely chopped Golden Delicious apples
½ cup broken pecans

2 cups miniature marshmallows

Mix first four ingredients in a glass bowl. Cover and refrigerate until chilled. Stir in marshmallows just before serving. Refrigerate leftovers.

Makes 8 servings.

SPINACH-APPLE SALAD

Add grilled chicken, cooked crisp bacon, sliced red onions and cubed avocado to this salad to make a delicious main course.

1 10-ounce package fresh spinach, torn
2 Granny Smith apples, unpeeled, cored and chopped
½ cup cashews
¼ cup golden raisins

Dressing
¼ cup granulated sugar
¼ cup apple cider vinegar
¼ cup vegetable oil
¼ teaspoon garlic salt
¼ teaspoon celery salt

Mix spinach, apples, cashews and raisins in a large glass bowl.

Dressing: Mix all dressing ingredients in a jar. Cover tightly and shake well. Pour dressing over salad. Toss to coat. Serve with warm hard rolls. Refrigerate leftovers.

Makes 6 servings.

WALDORF APPLE SALAD

This is a classic version of the Waldorf salad...there are many variations.

**2 cups cored, unpeeled and coarsely chopped
   Braeburn or Gala apples
1 cup chopped celery
½ cup mayonnaise
⅓ cup coarsely chopped walnuts**

Mix all ingredients in a bowl until apples are coated. Serve chilled, over a bed of lettuce, if desired. Refrigerate leftovers.

Makes 4 servings.

WISCONSIN CARAMEL
APPLE-CRANBERRY SALAD

You'll find Wisconsin cranberries and apples in this sweet salad.

1 3-ounce package instant butterscotch pudding
1 8-ounce container frozen non-dairy whipped topping, thawed
1 8-ounce can crushed pineapple, including juice

3 cups cored, unpeeled chopped apples
1 cup miniature marshmallows
¼ cup dried cranberries
1 cup dry-roasted peanuts

Mix dry pudding mix, thawed whipped topping and pineapple with juice in a large glass bowl until well blended. Stir in remaining ingredients; mix well. Refrigerate and chill well before serving. Refrigerate leftovers.

Makes 6 servings.

APPLE BARLEY SOUP

Serve this healthy soup hot...thanks, Doris, for sharing this recipe.

2 tablespoons corn oil
2 large onions, thinly sliced

3½ cups vegetable stock
1½ cups apple juice or apple cider
⅓ cup pearl barley
2 large carrots, diced
¾ teaspoon dried thyme
¼ teaspoon dried marjoram
1 bay leaf

2 cups chopped apples
¼ cup minced fresh parsley
1 tablespoon fresh lemon juice

Heat corn oil in a 3-quart saucepot over medium heat. Add onions; stir and cook 5 minutes. Reduce heat to medium-low. Cover and cook, stirring often, until onions are browned, about 10 minutes.

Add stock, apple juice, barley, carrots, thyme, marjoram and bay leaf. Cover and cook until barley is tender, about 1 hour.

Add apples, parsley and lemon juice. Cook until apples are tender, about 5 minutes. Discard bay leaf. Refrigerate leftovers.

Makes 4 servings.

CARROT-APPLE SOUP

Swirl a tablespoon of whipping cream into soup when serving, and garnish with fresh chives.

2 tablespoons margarine or butter
1 large onion, chopped

3 Golden Delicious apples, peeled, cored and cut into chunks
2 pounds carrots, peeled and cut into chunks
2 14-ounce cans chicken broth
1 tablespoon granulated sugar
1 teaspoon salt
1 teaspoon freshly grated peeled ginger
2 cups water

Melt margarine in a large soup pot over medium heat. Add onion; stir and cook until tender and golden, about 10 minutes.

Add remaining ingredients. Bring to a boil over high heat. Reduce heat to low. Cover and simmer 20 minutes or until carrots are tender. Remove from heat. Puree mixture until very smooth. Serve hot. Refrigerate leftovers.

Makes 8 servings.

CURRIED APPLE-CAULIFLOWER SOUP

Serve a cup of this soup with a favorite cold meat sandwich.

1½ tablespoons butter
½ cup finely chopped onion
2 large cloves garlic, minced
½ teaspoon curry powder

2½ cups chicken broth
1 large Granny Smith apple, peeled, cored and coarsely chopped
4 cups cauliflower florets

¼ cup whipping cream
salt and ground black pepper to taste

Add butter, onion, garlic and curry powder to a large saucepot. Cook and stir over medium-low heat until onions are softened.

Add broth, apple and cauliflower. Cover and simmer until cauliflower is very tender, about 20 minutes. Remove from heat. Puree mixture in batches in a food processor until smooth. Place mixture into a large saucepan. Stir in cream, salt and pepper. Heat soup until hot. Serve. Refrigerate leftovers.

Makes 4 servings.

GOUDA CHEESE APPLE SOUP

Serve hot in small bowls.

⅓ cup butter or margarine
⅓ cup all-purpose flour
½ teaspoon salt
2½ cups whole milk
4 cups Gouda cheese, shredded
1 cup apple juice

Melt butter in a saucepan over low heat. Stir in flour and salt until blended. Gradually add milk, stirring constantly, until mixture thickens. Stir in cheese until melted. Stir in apple juice; heat thoroughly. Refrigerate leftovers.

Makes 4 servings.

YAM-APPLE SOUP

When serving, garnish with whipped cream and a sprinkle of nutmeg.

¼ cup butter
1 medium onion, chopped
2 cups yams, peeled and chopped
1 cup peeled, cored and chopped apples
3 cups chicken stock
¼ cup maple syrup
½ teaspoon dried leaf thyme
salt and ground black pepper to taste

Melt butter in a saucepan over medium heat. Add onions; stir and cook 3 minutes. Add remaining ingredients. Bring to a boil, then reduce heat and simmer uncovered until yams and apples are tender, about 30 minutes. Puree mixture in a food processor or blender. Return to saucepot and heat thoroughly. Serve hot. Refrigerate leftovers.

Makes 4 servings.

Meals
Paired with
Apples

APPLE CHEESE STRATA

Serve this tasty dish for a special weekend breakfast.

12 slices firm day-old white bread, crusts removed
1 pound bulk pork sausage, cooked and drained
2 Golden Delicious apples, cored, peeled and thinly sliced
12 slices sharp cheddar cheese

4 eggs
2 cups whole milk
¼ teaspoon ground black pepper
⅛ teaspoon salt
⅛ teaspoon ground nutmeg

Arrange 6 bread slices into a greased 13x9x2-inch baking pan. Top with half of sausage, half of apples and half of cheese. Repeat layers.

Whisk remaining ingredients with a wire whisk in a medium bowl until well blended. Pour over layered mixture in baking pan. Press bread lightly to cover completely with egg mixture. Cover with plastic food wrap; refrigerate at least 4 hours or overnight.

Preheat oven to 350°.
Remove plastic wrap from baking pan. Bake uncovered 50–60 minutes or until a knife inserted in center comes out clean. Let stand a few minutes before serving. Serve warm. Refrigerate leftovers.

Makes 8 servings.

APPLE CINNAMON QUESADILLAS

Serve these quesadillas hot from the skillet for a special breakfast.

1 McIntosh apple, cored, peeled and chopped
¾ cup unsweetened applesauce
⅛ teaspoon ground cinnamon
4 6-inch flour tortillas
¼ cup shredded cheddar cheese

Yogurt dipping sauce
½ cup vanilla-flavored yogurt
2 tablespoons applesauce
pinch of ground cinnamon

Mix chopped apple, applesauce and cinnamon in a small bowl. Spoon half of apple mixture onto a tortilla; sprinkle with half the cheese. Top with another tortilla. Repeat with remaining tortillas, apple mixture and cheese.

Spray a large nonstick skillet with cooking spray; heat over medium until hot. Cook quesadillas, one at a time, about 2 minutes on each side or until golden brown. Remove from skillet; cut each into 4 wedges. Mix all yogurt dipping sauce ingredients and serve with quesadillas. Refrigerate leftovers.

Makes 4 servings.

APPLE SAGE BREAKFAST SAUSAGE

Serve with scrambled eggs…or serve patties on hot buttered biscuits for a delicious breakfast treat.

1 teaspoon corn oil
2 tablespoons finely chopped onion
1 Granny Smith apple, peeled, cored and finely diced
3 cloves garlic, finely chopped
½ teaspoon dried leaf thyme, crumbled
½ teaspoon ground ginger
1 teaspoon dried sage leaf, crumbled
¼ teaspoon salt
¼ teaspoon black pepper

1 pound fresh pork sausage meat
1 egg white

Heat corn oil in a large nonstick skillet. Add onion and apple; cook over medium heat, stirring occasionally, until softened, about 3 minutes. Stir in garlic, thyme, ginger, sage, salt and black pepper. Remove from heat; cool to room temperature in a large bowl.

Add sausage and egg white to cooled apple mixture in a large bowl. Shape into 12 equal patties. Cook patties in the same skillet, a few at a time if necessary, over medium heat until browned and cooked through, about 3–4 minutes per side. Serve warm. Refrigerate leftovers.

Makes 4 servings.

APPLE PECAN OVEN PANCAKE

Serve topped with softened butter and warm maple syrup, along with crisp bacon and hot coffee.

1 large apple, peeled, cored and chopped
⅓ cup chopped pecans, lightly toasted
½ cup granulated sugar, divided
2 teaspoons ground cinnamon, divided
3 teaspoons pure vanilla extract, divided

2 cups all-purpose baking mix
1 cup whole milk
2 large eggs, beaten

Preheat oven to 350°.
Grease a 10-inch pie plate.

Mix apple, pecans, 2 tablespoons sugar, 1 teaspoon cinnamon and 1 teaspoon vanilla in a small bowl; set aside.

Stir baking mix, milk, eggs, remaining sugar, 1 teaspoon cinnamon and 2 teaspoons vanilla in a large bowl until blended. Stir in apple mixture.

Pour batter into prepared pie plate. Bake about 40 minutes, or until a knife inserted in center comes out clean. Cut into wedges and serve immediately. Refrigerate leftovers.

Makes 8 servings.

APPLESAUCE WAFFLES

Serve these warm applesauce waffles with soft butter, maple syrup and sausage patties for a delicious breakfast or light supper.

1½ **cups all-purpose flour**
2 **tablespoons granulated sugar**
2 **teaspoons baking powder**
½ **teaspoon salt**
½ **teaspoon ground cinnamon**
¼ **teaspoon ground nutmeg**

2 **large eggs, separated**
1 **cup whole milk**
⅓ **cup corn oil**
¾ **cup applesauce**

Blend first six ingredients in a large bowl.

In another bowl, whisk egg yolks, milk and corn oil. Stir in applesauce; stir into dry mixture until well moistened. Whip egg whites in a bowl until soft peaks form; fold into batter. The batter will be thick.

Preheat waffle iron; when hot, brush the grids lightly with corn oil. Pour batter into the center of the waffle iron, gently spreading batter over the grid with a kitchen knife. Close the waffle iron and cook 3–4 minutes or until the steam escaping from sides is reduced. Remove cooked waffle with tines of a fork. Brush grids lightly with corn oil, and repeat process with remaining batter.

Makes 3 9-inch waffles.

BRIE APPLE OMELET

Serve with fruit juice, coffee and toast…buttered, of course. For variation, use ½ cup shredded cheddar cheese in place of Brie.

2 apples, peeled, cored and thinly sliced
8 tablespoons butter (1 stick)

8 eggs
3 tablespoons heavy cream
½ teaspoon salt
¼ teaspoon ground black pepper

2 tablespoons butter
8 tablespoons small cubes of Brie cheese

Stir and cook apples in 8 tablespoons butter until soft.

Beat eggs, cream, salt and pepper in a bowl until blended but not frothy.

Melt 2 tablespoons butter in omelet pan over high heat until it is almost changing color, but do not brown. Pour in egg mixture, beating with a fork to lighten, but still allowing mixture to settle on bottom of pan. Cook until bottom is light golden brown. Do not overcook. Fill omelet with cooked apples and cubed cheese. Fold omelet and slide it out of pan onto serving plate. Serve immediately.

Makes 4 servings.

GRUYERE APPLE FRITTATA

A good addition for a brunch. Substitute sharp cheddar cheese if desired.

5 eggs
½ teaspoon water
2 tablespoons butter
1 teaspoon corn oil
1 medium onion, chopped
2 medium Granny Smith apples, peeled, cored and finely chopped
½ teaspoon ground nutmeg
⅛ teaspoon white pepper
½ teaspoon salt or to taste
⅓ cup slivered almonds, lightly toasted
1½ tablespoons butter
1 cup shredded Gruyere cheese

Beat eggs and water in a large bowl until blended.

Melt 2 tablespoons butter and corn oil in a nonstick 10-inch skillet over medium-high heat. Add onion; stir and cook until lightly browned. Add apples; stir and cook 5 minutes. Spoon into egg mixture. Stir in nutmeg, pepper, salt and almonds.

Melt 1½ tablespoons butter in same skillet over medium-high heat. Pour in egg mixture; shake skillet to evenly distribute. Cook 1 minute, then sprinkle with cheese. Reduce heat to medium-low and cook about 11 minutes. Loosen the frittata, making sure it is detached from skillet. Place a large serving plate over skillet and invert onto plate. Put frittata back in skillet to cook the other side for 5 minutes. Remove from skillet to serving plate. Cut into wedges. Refrigerate leftovers.

Makes 4 servings.

OVEN APPLE FRENCH TOAST

A good dish to prepare the night before for brunch. Serve with crisp bacon, fruit juice and hot coffee.

1 cup brown sugar
½ cup butter, melted
2 teaspoons ground cinnamon, divided

3 Granny Smith apples, peeled, cored and sliced
½ cup raisins
1 loaf French bread cut in 1-inch-thick slices

6 large eggs
1½ cups whole milk
1 teaspoon pure vanilla extract

Mix sugar, butter and 1 teaspoon cinnamon in a small bowl; spoon into a 13x9-inch baking pan. Place apples and raisins on top of sugar mixture. Arrange 12 slices bread over apple-raisin layer.

Beat eggs, milk, vanilla and 1 teaspoon cinnamon in a bowl; pour over bread. Cover and refrigerate overnight or up to 24 hours.

Preheat oven to 375°.
Remove from refrigerator; cover with aluminum baking foil and bake 40 minutes. Remove foil and bake 5 minutes. Let stand 5 minutes before serving. Refrigerate leftovers.

Makes 12 servings.

SOUR CREAM APPLE PANCAKES

Serve with warm maple syrup and softened butter.

1½ cups all-purpose flour
¼ cup granulated sugar
1½ teaspoons baking powder
½ teaspoon baking soda
¾ teaspoon salt
½ teaspoon ground cinnamon

1½ cups dairy sour cream
½ cup whole milk
2 large eggs, beaten
¼ cup butter or margarine, melted and cooled
1 teaspoon pure vanilla extract

2 medium apples, peeled, cored and grated

Whisk first six ingredients in a large bowl until well blended.

Whisk sour cream, milk, eggs, butter and vanilla in another bowl; stir into flour mixture until well moistened. Stir in grated apples.

Grease a pancake griddle with corn oil and heat over medium-high heat until hot. Pour ¼ cup batter for each pancake onto hot griddle. Cook until small bubbles form around outside edges. Turn pancakes over and cook other side.

Add more milk to batter if necessary to maintain desired pouring consistency.

Makes 12 pancakes.

APPLE BUTTER GRILLED PORK COUNTRY RIBS

Serve with green salad, corn on the cob and crusty bread.

**2 pounds country-style pork loin ribs, lightly seasoned with
salt and ground black pepper**

½ cup apple butter
½ cup honey barbecue sauce
½ cup finely chopped yellow onion

Preheat oven to 350°.
Place ribs in an ungreased 13x9x2-inch baking pan. Cover with cooking foil. Bake 1 hour.

Stir apple butter, barbecue sauce and onions in a small saucepan. Bring to a boil over medium heat, stirring often. Reduce heat; cover and simmer 15 minutes; remove from heat; set aside.

Heat grill. Brush 1 side of ribs with apple butter mixture. Place ribs, apple butter mixture side down on heated grill. Brush tops of ribs with mixture; cook until ribs are browned, about 15 minutes, turning and brushing occasionally with apple butter mixture. Bring remaining apple butter mixture to a boil in a clean saucepan; serve with hot ribs. Refrigerate leftovers.

Makes 4 servings.

APPLE CHICKEN STIR-FRY

The apple gives the stir-fry a tangy crunch.

2½ tablespoons corn oil, divided
1 pound boneless, skinless, chicken breast, cubed

½ cup onion, vertically sliced
1 cup carrots, thinly sliced

1 teaspoon dried basil, crushed

1 cup fresh or frozen Chinese pea pods
1 tablespoon water
1 medium size Fuji apple, cored and thinly sliced

Heat 1 tablespoon corn oil in a nonstick skillet over medium-high heat. Add chicken; cook and stir until chicken is no longer pink and juices run clear; remove from skillet.

Heat remaining corn oil in same skillet over medium-high heat. Add onion and carrots; cook and stir until carrots are tender. Stir in basil. Add pea pods and water; cook and stir 2 minutes. Return chicken to skillet; heat through. Remove from heat. Stir in apples. Serve hot over hot cooked and buttered white or brown rice. Refrigerate leftovers.

Makes 4 servings.

APPLE HAM CHEDDAR SOURDOUGH SANDWICHES

Serve with a bowl of creamy tomato soup.

2 tablespoons soft butter
8 ¼-inch-thick slices sourdough bread
4 slices fully cooked ham
1 small Granny Smith apple, cut into ¼-inch slices
6 ounces medium or sharp cheddar cheese, coarsely grated

Butter one side of each slice of bread. Place a slice of ham on unbuttered side of 4 bread slices. Top with four apple slices per sandwich, cheese and remaining four bread slices, buttered side up.

Heat a large nonstick skillet over medium-high heat two minutes. Put sandwiches in skillet (in batches if necessary), cover and cook two minutes or until undersides are golden brown and cheese has begun to melt. Uncover and carefully flip each sandwich, using a spatula, pressing to flatten slightly. Cook one minute or until undersides are golden brown. Carefully flip sandwich again, press with spatula and cook 30 seconds or until cheese is completely melted. Serve immediately. Refrigerate leftovers.

Makes 4 servings.

APPLE PORK CURRY

Serve pork chops and sauce over cooked rice or hot cooked couscous, flavored with chopped green onions and raisins.

2 tablespoons olive oil
4 boneless pork chops, trimmed

1 small onion, sliced
2 cloves garlic, minced
1 Granny Smith apple, peeled, cored and sliced
1 small red bell pepper, seeded and cut into thin strips

½ cup chicken stock
1 teaspoon cornstarch
1 teaspoon curry powder
½ teaspoon ground cumin
½ teaspoon ground cinnamon
salt and ground black pepper to taste

Heat oil in a heavy skillet over medium-high heat. Add pork chops; cook until browned on both sides and almost cooked through; remove from pan and set aside. Add onion, garlic, apple and bell pepper to same skillet; stir and cook until softened, about 2 minutes.

Mix chicken stock and cornstarch in a cup; stir into skillet. Stir in remaining ingredients except salt and black pepper. Cook and stir until slightly reduced and thickened. Return pork chops to skillet; adjust seasoning with salt and pepper. Cook until heated through, about 2 minutes. Serve warm. Refrigerate leftovers.

Makes 4 servings.

BEEF AND APPLE STIR-FRY

Serve alone or with hot steamed white rice.

2½ teaspoons soy sauce
1¼ teaspoons cornstarch
1 pound flank steak, cut into ½-inch cubes
½ teaspoon freshly grated lemon zest
1¼ tablespoons fresh lemon juice
¼ teaspoon Chinese five-spice powder
1 large Granny Smith apple, unpeeled, cored and
  cut into ½-inch cubes
4 green onions, cut into 2-inch pieces
1½ tablespoons corn oil
½ green bell pepper, cut into ½-inch pieces
½ red bell pepper, cut into ½-inch pieces

Mix soy sauce and cornstarch. Add meat and stir until coated. Allow meat to marinate 10 minutes.

Stir lemon zest, juice and spice in another bowl. Stir in apples until coated; set aside.

Heat a stir-fry pan over high heat until very hot. Add corn oil, then swirl oil to coat pan. Add meat; stir and cook about 2 minutes for rare, or longer for well done. Add apple mixture, green onions and bell peppers. Cook and stir until apples are just tender-crisp, about 2 minutes. Serve immediately. Refrigerate leftovers.

Makes 4 servings.

BRIE APPLE BAKED CHICKEN BREASTS

Serve with a green salad and rice pilaf.

2 tablespoons corn oil
1 medium onion, chopped
1 Granny Smith apple, cored, peeled and coarsely chopped
1 teaspoon dried thyme, divided
1 teaspoon salt, divided
½ teaspoon ground black pepper, divided
¾ cup apple cider, divided
4 ounces Brie cheese, rind removed, cut into chunks
4 medium size chicken breast halves with bone and skin

Heat corn oil in a medium nonstick skillet over medium heat. Add onion; stir and cook until very tender. Add apple, ½ teaspoon thyme, ¼ teaspoon salt, ¼ teaspoon black pepper and ¼ cup apple cider. Cook, stirring occasionally, until apple is tender. Remove from heat, cool slightly; stir in cheese.

Divide apple mixture into 4 equal portions. Run fingers under skin of chicken breast to detach from flesh. Put a portion of apple mixture under skin of each breast; distribute evenly. Season chicken with ¼ teaspoon salt and ¼ teaspoon black pepper; place in a greased 13x9x2-inch baking dish.

Preheat oven to 400°.
Bake about 35 minutes, until chicken is no longer pink near bone, and an instant-read meat thermometer registers 180°. Skim fat from baking dish. Scrape drippings into a small saucepan. Add ½ cup apple cider; cook over medium heat until mixture is reduced by half. Stir in ½ teaspoon thyme and ¼ teaspoon salt. Spoon over chicken. Serve warm. Refrigerate leftovers.

Makes 4 servings.

CHICKEN TACOS WITH APPLES

Soft chicken tacos flavored with tart apple.

1 tablespoon corn oil
1 pound boneless, skinless chicken breasts, cut into bite-size pieces
½ teaspoon salt
½ teaspoon ground black pepper
½ teaspoon ground nutmeg

1 tablespoon butter
2 cups thinly sliced onion
2 cups thinly sliced peeled Granny Smith apples
2 cloves garlic, minced

8 6-inch flour tortillas

Heat corn oil in a large nonstick skillet over medium-high heat. Season chicken with salt, pepper and nutmeg; add to skillet. Stir and cook chicken about 7 minutes or until no longer pink, and color is golden. Remove from skillet; keep warm.

Melt butter in same skillet over medium heat. Add onion; stir and cook until tender, about 4 minutes. Add apples; stir and cook about 6 minutes or until golden. Add garlic; stir and cook 30 seconds. Return chicken to skillet; stir until heated.

Heat tortillas according to package directions. Spoon ½ cup chicken mixture over each tortilla. Serve immediately. Refrigerate leftovers.

Makes 4 servings.

HONEY MUSTARD PORK ROAST WITH APPLE STUFFING

Serve with mashed potatoes and steamed broccoli.

½ cup chopped onion
¼ cup chopped celery
3 tablespoons butter or margarine

½ cup honey mustard, divided
2½ cups white bread cubes
⅔ cup cored, unpeeled and chopped
  Granny Smith apple
½ teaspoon poultry seasoning

1 3-pound boneless pork loin roast,
  butterfly cut
1 tablespoon all-purpose flour
1 cup unsweetened apple juice
2 tablespoons chopped fresh parsley

Preheat oven to 325°.
Stir and cook onion and celery in margarine in a large skillet over medium-high heat until crisp-tender. Remove from heat. Add 2 tablespoons honey mustard, bread cubes, apple and poultry seasoning; mix well.

Unroll pork loin roast. Spread with 2 tablespoons mustard; top with bread mixture. Re-roll pork loin roast and secure with kitchen string. Place on a rack in a roasting pan. Bake 2 hours or until a meat thermometer inserted into thickest part of roast registers 160°. Remove roast from pan to a carving board. Let stand 10 minutes before slicing and serving.

Add 1 tablespoon of drippings from roasting pan to a small saucepan; whisk in flour until well blended. Stir and cook 1 minute. Stir in apple juice and remaining ¼ cup mustard; cook and stir until mixture thickens and begins to boil. Remove from heat; stir in parsley. Slice the roast and serve warm, topped with warm mustard sauce. Refrigerate leftovers.

Makes 12 servings.

PORK APPLE WRAPS

Marinated pork with fresh apple salsa.

Salsa
1 teaspoon granulated sugar
1 teaspoon fresh lime juice
2 Granny Smith apples,
  cored and diced
½ ripe avocado, peeled and diced
1 tablespoon diced green onion,
  including tops
1 teaspoon chopped fresh cilantro leaves
½ teaspoon minced fresh jalapeno pepper
¼ teaspoon minced garlic
salt to taste

8 ounces pork tenderloin
salt and ground black pepper
8 8-inch flour tortillas, warmed

Marinade
1 tablespoon vegetable oil
2 tablespoons water
2 tablespoons fresh lime juice
3 large cloves garlic, finely
  minced
1 teaspoon minced fresh cilantro
¼ teaspoon red pepper flakes

Salsa: Mix all salsa ingredients in a glass bowl; cover and refrigerate 2 hours.

Marinade: Mix all marinade ingredients in a small glass bowl.

Season pork with salt and pepper. Place in a shallow pan; pour marinade over. Cover and refrigerate 1½ hours, turning occasionally. Drain pork; reserve marinade. Place pork on a rack in a shallow roasting pan. Brush with marinade.

Preheat oven to 375°.
Bake about 30 minutes or until meat tests done. Cut pork diagonally across grain into thin slices; place equal portions on each warm tortilla. Spoon 2 tablespoons salsa in center of each. Fold bottom half of tortilla over filling and overlap sides on top. Serve warm. Pass around remaining salsa. Refrigerate leftovers.

Makes 4 servings.

PORK TENDERLOIN WITH APPLES

Serve with steamed potatoes, buttered green beans and crusty bread.

3 tablespoons corn oil, divided
1 pound pork tenderloin, seasoned lightly with salt and ground black pepper
2 tablespoons grainy Dijon-type mustard
2 teaspoons fennel seeds

1 large yellow onion, sliced
2 Granny Smith apples, peeled, cored and sliced ¼-inch thick

½ cup apple cider

Preheat oven to 450°.
Heat 2 tablespoons corn oil in a large nonstick ovenproof skillet over medium-high heat. Add pork; brown on all sides. Remove from skillet to a plate; cool slightly. Spread mustard over top and sides of pork. Press fennel seeds into mustard.

Heat 1 tablespoon corn oil in same skillet. Add onion and apples; stir and cook over medium heat until golden, about 5 minutes. Smooth mixture evenly in skillet; sprinkle lightly with salt and ground black pepper. Place pork on top of apple mixture.

Bake until a meat thermometer registers 150° when inserted in center of pork. Remove pork to a serving platter. Cut diagonally into ½-inch-thick slices; keep warm.

Add cider to apple mixture in skillet; stir over high heat until slightly reduced. Spoon mixture onto individual plates; top with pork and serve. Refrigerate leftovers.

Makes 4 servings.

SLOW COOKER APPLE PORK TENDERLOINS

Serve with hot cooked white rice along with a green salad.

1 2-pound pork tenderloin
1 large onion, halved and cut into ¼-inch slices
2 medium tart cooking apples, peeled, cored and coarsely chopped
2 tablespoons apple jelly
1 tablespoon cider vinegar
salt and coarsely ground black pepper to taste

Brown pork tenderloin in corn oil in a skillet over medium heat. Remove from skillet and place in slow cooker. Add remaining ingredients to slow cooker, cover and cook on low heat setting for 7–9 hours.

Makes 6 servings.

TURKEY BREAST WITH SAUSAGE APPLE STUFFING

Sausage, pecans, apple and apricots in this stuffed turkey.

1 pound bulk pork sausage

2 cups dried bread cubes
1 cup pecan halves
¼ cup dried apple rings, re-hydrated, chopped
½ cup chopped dried apricots
¼ cup butter, melted
⅓ cup chicken broth

1 cup sliced celery
½ cup chopped onion
½ teaspoon salt
⅛ teaspoon ground black pepper
¼ teaspoon dried sage leaves, crushed

1 6-pound bone-in turkey breast
3 tablespoons butter, melted

Preheat oven to 350°.
Stir and cook sausage in a 10-inch skillet over medium heat until browned; drain fat. Place sausage in a large bowl. Add remaining ingredients except turkey and 3 tablespoons melted butter; mix well. Loosen skin from turkey and stuff with some of the sausage mixture. Secure skin with toothpicks.

Spoon remaining sausage mixture into a 1-quart covered baking dish; refrigerate until ready to bake. Bake during the last 30–40 minutes of turkey baking time until thoroughly heated and vegetables are tender.

Place stuffed turkey breast, breast-side up, on a rack in a roasting pan. Brush with 3 tablespoons melted butter. Bake, basting occasionally, 2–2½ hours or until a meat thermometer registers 175° and turkey breast is no longer pink. Let stand a few minutes before serving. Refrigerate leftovers.

Makes 8 servings.

Stuffing
Sides

ALMOND BROWN RICE APPLE STUFFING

For a variation, add 2 cups sliced mushrooms to the apples.

⅛ **cup slivered almonds**
2 **teaspoons margarine**
2 **medium tart apples, cored and diced**
½ **cup chopped onion**
½ **cup chopped celery**
½ **teaspoon poultry seasoning**
¼ **teaspoon dried thyme leaves, crushed**
¼ **teaspoon ground black pepper**
3 **cups cooked brown rice (cooked in chicken broth instead of water)**

Stir and cook almonds in margarine in a large skillet over medium-high heat until brown. Add apples, onion, celery, poultry seasoning, thyme and pepper; cook until apples are tender-crisp. Stir in cooked rice and heat through.

Use stuffing for chicken or pork roast. Stuffing may be baked in a covered baking dish at 375° for 15–20 minutes. Serve hot. Refrigerate leftovers.

Makes 6 servings.

APPLE PECAN BAKED STUFFING

Enjoy this stuffing plain, or use it to stuff an 8–10 pound turkey.

1 cup chicken broth
½ cup chopped celery
⅓ cup chopped onion
4 tablespoons butter
½ teaspoon salt

4 cups dry wheat bread cubes, about 8 slices
2 medium apples, peeled, cored and finely chopped
½ cup chopped pecans
1 teaspoon ground sage
¼ teaspoon ground cinnamon
⅛ teaspoon ground black pepper

Preheat oven to 350°.
Bring broth, celery, onion, butter and salt to a boil in a small saucepan.
Reduce heat; cover and simmer until vegetables are tender, about 5 minutes.

Mix remaining ingredients in a large bowl; add broth mixture. Gently stir to moisten. Spoon into a buttered 1½ quart casserole-baking dish. Cover and bake 25–30 minutes. Serve hot. Refrigerate leftovers.

Makes 6 servings.

CRANBERRY-APPLE STUFFING

Rosemary, parsley and thyme in this good stuffing.

½ cup butter
2 cups chopped celery
1 large onion, chopped

1 teaspoon dried thyme leaves
1 teaspoon dried parsley flakes
½ teaspoon dried rosemary leaves
1 cup dried cranberries
2 McIntosh apples, unpeeled, cored and chopped
1 teaspoon freshly grated orange peel, optional

4 cups unseasoned dry bread cubes
1 cup chicken broth

Preheat oven to 325°.
Melt butter in a large saucepan over medium heat. Add celery and onion; stir and cook 5 minutes. Remove from heat. Stir in thyme, parsley, rosemary, cranberries, apples and orange peel.

Place bread cubes in a large bowl. Stir in apple mixture, then stir in broth until combined. Spoon into a lightly buttered 13x9x2-inch baking dish. Cover and bake 35–40 minutes. Serve hot. Refrigerate leftovers.

Makes 8 servings.

FRESH APPLE-CRANBERRY CORN BREAD STUFFING

Use this to stuff a turkey instead of baking in a casserole dish, if desired.

1 cup sweetened dried cranberries
1½ cups hot chicken broth
3 tablespoons butter
2 cups coarsely chopped unpeeled Ida Red or Rome Beauty apples
1 cup chopped onions
1 6-ounce package cornbread stuffing mix

Preheat oven to 350°.
Mix cranberries and hot broth in a bowl; mix well. Melt butter in a large saucepan over medium heat. Add apples and onions; cook and stir until onions are soft, about 8 minutes. Stir in stuffing mix and cranberry broth mixture until moistened. Spoon into a greased 2-quart glass baking dish. Bake 15–20 minutes or until stuffing is very hot. Refrigerate leftovers.

Makes 8 servings.

HERB APPLE AND SAUSAGE CORN BREAD STUFFING

Herbs, apples and sausage in this baked stuffing.

1 pound bulk pork sausage or bulk Italian sausage

½ cup butter
1 large yellow onion, chopped
1 cup chopped celery
2 Granny Smith apples, peeled, cored and cut into ½-inch cubes
3 tablespoons chopped fresh sage (or ½ teaspoon ground dried)
½ teaspoon dried thyme leaves, crumbled
¼ teaspoon ground black pepper
salt to taste

5 cups coarse corn bread crumbs corn bread croutons
5 cups white bread croutons, purchased or homemade
2 cups chicken broth

Preheat oven to 375°.
Cook and stir sausage in a saucepan until no longer pink; drain fat. Place sausage in a large bowl; set aside.

Melt butter in same saucepan over medium heat. Add onion and celery; cook and stir until softened. Add apple; cook and stir until softened. Stir in sage, thyme, black pepper and salt; spoon into large bowl with sausage. Add croutons and broth; mix well. Spoon into a greased 3-quart baking dish. Bake 30–40 minutes. Serve warm. Refrigerate leftovers.

Makes 8 servings.

SAUSAGE APPLE CHESTNUT STUFFING

A special stuffing for holidays. Makes 12 cups, enough for a 16-lb. turkey.

1 pound firm white bread, crusts
  removed, cut into ½-inch cubes
¾ pound bulk pork sausage

4 tablespoons butter
1 large yellow onion, chopped
3 large celery stalks, chopped
2 large Granny Smith apples,
  peeled, cored and chopped
3 tablespoons chopped fresh thyme
  (or 2 teaspoons dried)

¾ cup chicken broth
1 pound fresh chestnuts, baked
  and peeled, or 2 cups vacuum-
  packed, peeled, jarred chestnuts
½ cup chopped fresh flat leaf
  parsley
2 eggs, slightly beaten
salt and ground black pepper
  to taste

Preheat oven to 400°.
Place bread cubes in a large baking pan. Bake, stirring occasionally, until
lightly golden, about 12 minutes. Remove from pan; pour into a large bowl;
set aside. Cook and stir sausage in a skillet over medium heat until
browned, about 10 minutes. Using a slotted spoon, remove sausage from
skillet, place into bowl with bread.

Add butter to drippings in skillet. Add onion and celery; stir and cook until
tender. Add apples and thyme; stir and cook 2 minutes. Remove all from
skillet, leaving the drippings, and place into bowl with bread mixture.

Stir broth in skillet; bring to a boil. Stir into bread mixture. Add remaining
ingredients; mix well.

Reduce oven to 325°. Spoon stuffing into a buttered 13x9-inch baking dish.
Bake, covered with cooking foil, 30 minutes. Uncover and bake until top is
crisp, about 25 minutes. Serve hot. Refrigerate leftovers. Makes 6 servings.

ACORN SQUASH WITH APPLE STUFFING

A great side to dress up those grilled burgers.

3 acorn squash, cut lengthwise, seeds discarded
2 tablespoons maple syrup, divided

½ cup chopped walnuts
2 teaspoons corn oil
1 large onion, finely chopped
1 large stalk celery, thinly sliced
1 Granny Smith apple, peeled, cored and cut into ¼-inch cubes
⅓ cup golden raisins, chopped
¼ cup uncooked bulgur wheat
¾ cup chicken broth
¼ teaspoon ground cinnamon
⅛ teaspoon salt

Preheat oven to 400°.
Grease a 15x10x1-inch baking pan.
Brush cut surfaces and inside of squash with 1 tablespoon syrup. Place squash cut-side down on prepared pan. Bake 30–40 minutes, until tender.

Stir walnuts in a nonstick skillet over medium heat until lightly toasted; remove and set aside. Heat corn oil in same skillet over medium heat; add onion and celery; stir and cook just until tender, about 3 minutes. Add remaining ingredients. Cover and simmer 15 minutes or until bulgur is tender and liquid absorbed. Stir in toasted walnuts.

Reduce heat to 375°. Turn squash cut-side up. Fill with apple mixture and drizzle with remaining syrup. Bake 15 minutes

Makes 6 servings.

APPLE CIDER BAKED BEANS

Instead of dried beans, you can use three 15-ounce cans navy beans or great northern beans, drained and rinsed.

2 cups dried white navy beans

1 medium onion, diced
4 tablespoons molasses
8 teaspoons Dijon-type mustard
2 tablespoons tomato paste
½ teaspoon salt
1 teaspoon ground black pepper
2 teaspoons dried thyme
1 small bay leaf
1 teaspoon cider vinegar
4 teaspoons soy sauce
1⅓ cups apple cider, boiling

Pick beans over and discard broken pieces. Wash beans in cold water twice. Place beans in a large nonreactive pot. Cover beans with 3 inches of cold water. Soak 8–10 hours.

Preheat oven to 250°.
Drain beans; reserve liquid. Bring liquid to a boil in a saucepan; set aside. Place beans in a deep 3-quart baking dish. Add remaining ingredients to beans, and enough reserved boiled liquid to cover beans; stir. Cover and bake 6 hours, adding a little more water if necessary after 3 hours baking. Serve hot. Refrigerate leftovers.

Makes 6 servings.

APPLE RINGS AND YAMS

Sweet potatoes may be used instead of yams.

2 large yams, baked, peeled and sliced crosswise
2 Golden Delicious apples, cored, peeled and sliced
crosswise into rings

¼ cup brown sugar, packed
1 teaspoon cornstarch
⅛ teaspoon ground cloves
½ cup fresh orange juice
½ teaspoon pure vanilla extract
2 tablespoons chopped pecans or walnuts

Preheat oven to 350°.
Layer yam and apple slices alternately in a shallow, buttered 1-quart
baking dish.

Mix sugar, cornstarch and cloves in a small saucepan. Stir in orange juice
until smooth. Stir and cook mixture over medium heat until thickened. Stir
in vanilla. Pour over apple and yam slices. Top with pecans. Bake until
apples are tender, about 20 minutes. Serve hot. Refrigerate leftovers.

Makes 6 servings.

BRUSSELS SPROUTS WITH APPLES

Brussels sprouts with apples…a special side dish.

2 pounds fresh Brussels sprouts, halved
3 tablespoons fresh lemon juice
2 teaspoons salt, divided
water

¼ cup butter, divided
1 medium onion, diced
¼ cup apple juice
1 large unpeeled Red Delicious apple, cored and diced
1 clove garlic, minced
1 teaspoon granulated sugar
1 8-ounce can sliced water chestnuts, drained
½ cup golden raisins
2 teaspoons grated fresh lemon rind
½ teaspoon ground black pepper
⅛ teaspoon ground nutmeg

Place Brussels sprouts, lemon juice, 1½ teaspoons salt and enough water to cover in a saucepan. Bring to a boil. Reduce heat. Cover and simmer 5–10 minutes or until tender. Drain and keep warm.

Melt 2 tablespoons butter in a large skillet over medium-high heat. Add onion; stir and cook 10 minutes. Stir in juice; cook 2 minutes. Add apple, garlic and sugar; stir and cook until apples are tender. Stir in 2 tablespoons butter, ½ teaspoon salt and remaining ingredients. Stir and cook 3 minutes. Add warm Brussels sprouts; toss gently. Serve hot. Refrigerate leftovers.

Makes 6 servings.

CARROT-APPLE BAKE

Carrots and apples…a good side.

6 large carrots, peeled and thinly sliced
5 large Rome Beauty apples, peeled, cored and sliced

5 tablespoons granulated sugar
5 tablespoons all-purpose flour
½ teaspoon ground nutmeg
1 tablespoon butter or margarine, cut up
½ cup fresh orange juice

Preheat oven to 350°.
Cook carrots in lightly salted water in a saucepan 5 minutes; drain. Cook apples in unsalted water in a saucepan 5 minutes; drain.

Layer carrots and apples in a 2-quart buttered baking dish. Mix sugar, flour and nutmeg in a small bowl; sprinkle on top. Dot with butter. Pour orange juice over all. Bake 30–40 minutes or until apples are tender. Serve warm. Refrigerate leftovers.

Makes 6 servings.

MOOSE'S APPLE-SWEET POTATO-PINEAPPLE BAKE

A good side to serve with turkey or ham.

2 16-ounce cans sweet potatoes, drained
1⅓ cups canned French fried onions, divided
1 large apple, cored, peeled and sliced into thin wedges

2 8-ounce cans crushed pineapple, undrained
½ teaspoon pure vanilla extract
3 tablespoons light brown sugar, packed
½ teaspoon ground cinnamon

Preheat oven to 375°.
Grease a shallow 2-quart baking dish.

Layer sweet potatoes, ⅔ cup French fried onions and half of the apple wedges in prepared baking dish.

Mix pineapple (including liquid), vanilla, sugar and cinnamon in a medium bowl. Spoon over sweet potato mixture. Arrange remaining apple wedges over pineapple layer. Cover and bake 35 minutes or until heated through. Uncover; sprinkle with remaining ⅔ cup French fried onions. Bake 3 minutes or until onions are golden. Serve hot. Refrigerate leftovers.

Makes 6 servings.

RED CABBAGE WITH APPLES

Good side to serve with sausage or ham.

¼ cup corn oil
4 large Ida Red apples, peeled, cored and chopped
1 large onion, chopped
1 medium red cabbage, shredded
½ cup water

½ cup dark corn syrup
⅓ cup white vinegar
2 tablespoons butter or margarine
salt and ground black pepper to taste

Heat corn oil in a large pot. Add apples and onions; stir and cook over low heat 10 minutes. Add cabbage and water; cook 20 minutes, adding a little more water if necessary.

Add corn syrup and vinegar; cook 5 minutes. Stir in butter. Season with salt and pepper to taste. Serve warm. Refrigerate leftovers.

Makes 8 servings.

RUTH'S WHIPPED APPLE-SWEET POTATO BAKE

Whipped apples and sweet potatoes…a nice side.

3 cups peeled, cored and sliced apples such as McIntosh or Gala
3 cups cubed, peeled fresh sweet potatoes
1½ cups apple juice or apple cider

¼ teaspoon salt
½ teaspoon ground cinnamon
¼ teaspoon ground nutmeg
¼ teaspoon ground ginger
2 tablespoons butter or margarine
⅓ cup brown sugar, packed
2 cups miniature marshmallows, divided
⅓ cup chopped pecans

Preheat oven to 350°.
Place apples, sweet potatoes and apple juice in a 3-quart saucepan. Cover and cook over medium heat until tender, about 20 minutes. Drain.

Add salt, spices, butter and sugar to apple mixture. Whip with electric mixer or mash by hand until potatoes are smooth. Stir in 1 cup marshmallows. Spread hot mixture evenly into a shallow, buttered 1½-quart glass baking dish. Sprinkle with remaining marshmallows and pecans. Bake about 15 minutes or until marshmallows are melted and lightly browned. Serve hot. Refrigerate leftovers.

Makes 6 servings.

SCALLOPED APPLES WITH CRANBERRIES

Canned apple slices and apple pie filling makes this an easy dish to prepare. Serve with ham, turkey and other meat dishes.

1 20-ounce can apple slices
1 21-ounce can apple pie filling
¾ cup canned whole berry cranberry sauce
¼ cup chopped walnuts
½ cup brown sugar, packed
1 teaspoon ground cinnamon
½ teaspoon pure vanilla extract

Preheat oven to 350°.
Mix all ingredients in a large bowl. Spoon into a buttered 1½-quart baking dish. Bake about 30 minutes or until very hot and bubbly. Serve hot. Refrigerate leftovers.

Makes 8 servings.

SPICED APPLES

Serve over waffles topped with maple syrup, or as a side for pork roast and other meats.

½ **cup butter**
4 **large Granny Smith apples, peeled, cored and sliced**
4 **Golden Delicious apples, peeled, cored and sliced**
1½ **cups granulated sugar**
1 **teaspoon ground cinnamon**
½ **teaspoon ground nutmeg**

Melt butter in a large skillet over medium-high heat and add remaining ingredients. Stir and cook 15–20 minutes or until apples are tender. Serve warm. Refrigerate leftovers.

Makes 8 servings.

SWEET POTATOES WITH CHUNKY APPLESAUCE

Fresh sweet potatoes smothered in applesauce.

3 large fresh sweet potatoes
¼ cup butter
¼ cup brown sugar, mixed in a cup with ⅛ teaspoon salt
2 cups chunky applesauce

Preheat oven to 350°.
Peel sweet potatoes and cut into 1-inch cubes. Cook in a saucepan in rapidly boiling water for 15 minutes; drain. Place sweet potatoes in a 1½-quart greased baking dish. Dot with butter. Sprinkle with brown sugar mixture. Spoon applesauce over all. Bake until tender, about 30 minutes. Serve warm. Refrigerate leftovers.

Makes 6 servings.

Beverages

CITRUS CIDER PUNCH

Use ice cubes made with apple juice for a special touch. Garnish with fresh mint leaves when serving.

3 cups sweet apple cider or apple juice
2 cups orange juice
1 cup pineapple juice
1 6-ounce can frozen lemonade concentrate, do not thaw

2 quarts ginger ale
4 cups ice cubes

Mix first four ingredients in a large glass punch bowl until well blended.

Gradually stir in ginger ale and ice cubes. Serve immediately.

Makes about 20 cups.

HOT BUTTERED CIDER

Hot buttered cider…always a treat.

2 cups unfiltered apple cider
1 teaspoon Chinese five-spice powder
2 tablespoons honey
2 teaspoon unsalted butter, cut into small pieces

In a small saucepan, mix cider, spice and honey until blended; bring to a boil over medium heat. Reduce heat and simmer 1 minute. Remove from heat; stir in butter until melted.

Makes 2 servings.

HOT CIDER WASSAIL

On a frosty evening, serve a mug of this hot cider for a delightful treat.

8 cups apple cider
2 cups fresh orange juice
1 cup fresh lemon juice
5 cups pineapple juice
1 teaspoon whole cloves
2 cinnamon sticks

Mix all ingredients in a large pot. Bring to a simmer over medium heat.
Remove from heat; strain and serve hot.

Makes 20 servings.

SPICED APPLE TEA

Tea lover's treat!

6 cups apple cider
3 tablespoons pure lemon juice
½ cup brown sugar, packed
1 cinnamon stick
1 teaspoon whole cloves
½ teaspoon whole allspice
2 tea bags

In a 3-quart saucepan, mix apple cider, lemon juice and sugar. Tie spices in cheesecloth and add to saucepan. Bring mixture to a boil over medium heat, then reduce heat and simmer 5 minutes. Remove from heat. Add tea bags; steep 5 minutes. Discard spice bag and tea bags. Serve hot.

Makes 8 servings.

APPLE-RASPBERRY PUNCH

Raspberry sherbet, apple juice and frozen raspberries in this delicious punch.

1 pint raspberry sherbet

2 cups apple juice
2 cups water
1 cup fresh lemon juice
1 cup granulated sugar

1 10-ounce package frozen raspberries
1 28-ounce bottle grapefruit carbonated beverage
   or ginger ale, chilled

Spoon sherbet into a punch bowl.

Mix apple juice, water, lemon juice and sugar in a bowl until sugar is dissolved. Stir in raspberries. Pour mixture into punch bowl; stir. Slowly add carbonated beverage.

Makes 25 servings.

Sauces
Condiments

APPLE CIDER BARBECUE SAUCE

Good on ribs and chicken.

2 cups apple cider
3 cups apple cider vinegar
1 12-ounce can tomato puree
½ cup molasses
¾ cup brown sugar, packed
10 3-inch-long cinnamon sticks
8 dried hot chili peppers
1 teaspoon whole black peppercorns
½ teaspoon salt
6 cloves garlic, smashed
4 fresh bay leaves

Bring all ingredients to a boil in a saucepot. Reduce heat; simmer over medium-low heat until thickened, about 2 hours. Strain and discard solids. Spoon sauce into clean glass jars. Use or refrigerate up to 2 weeks.

Makes about 5 cups.

APPLESAUCE

This will be chunky applesauce; beat for a creamy consistency if desired.

4 peeled, cored and sliced Braeburn apples, or any tart sweet apple
½ cup water

⅓ cup granulated sugar
¼ teaspoon ground cinnamon
⅛ teaspoon ground nutmeg
½ teaspoon pure vanilla extract

Bring apples and water to a boil in a medium saucepan; reduce heat. Simmer uncovered, stirring occasionally, until apples are soft, about 10–15 minutes. Break up apples with a fork while cooking.

Stir in remaining ingredients; boil 1 minute. Serve or refrigerate.

Makes about 4 cups.

APPLE-CRANBERRY SAUCE

A special side for those holidays!

6 Spartan or Fuji apples, peeled, cored and diced
¼ cup fresh orange juice
1 tablespoon fresh lemon juice

2 cups fresh cranberries
¾ teaspoon ground cinnamon
¼ teaspoon ground ginger
⅛ teaspoon ground cloves
⅓ cup granulated sugar

Place apples, orange juice and lemon juice in a medium saucepan. Cook over low heat until apples are tender. Remove from heat and mash apples with a fork. Add remaining ingredients. Stir and cook until cranberries are soft. Remove from heat. Serve warm or cold. Refrigerate leftovers.

Makes 8 servings.

MICROWAVE THREE-APPLE APPLESAUCE

Stir in a pinch of ground cinnamon if desired.

2 Granny Smith apples, peeled, cored and thinly sliced
2 Fuji apples, peeled, cored and thinly sliced
2 Golden Delicious apples, peeled, cored and thinly sliced
¼ cup water
1 tablespoon granulated sugar

Place sliced apples in a large microwave-safe bowl. Add water. Cover with plastic food wrap; microwave on high for 10 minutes. Uncover and stir apples; microwave uncovered until apples are very tender, about 5 minutes. Add sugar and coarsely mash apples with a fork. Serve or store in a glass container in refrigerator.

Makes about 3½ cups.

APPLE CHUTNEY

This is a delicious chutney…serve with lamb, pork or duck.

8 cups peeled, cored, coarsely chopped apples
2 cups chopped dried apricots
7 tablespoons chopped instant onions
1 pound brown sugar
1 pint vinegar
1 tablespoon ground ginger
1 tablespoon dried mint flakes
2 teaspoons ground allspice
2 teaspoons salt
1 tablespoon mustard seed
1 teaspoon cayenne or red pepper
pinch instant minced garlic

Mix all ingredients in a large nonreactive saucepan. Bring to a boil, then lower heat and simmer 1 hour or until mixture is thickened. Immediately fill hot sterilized jars, leaving ½-inch headspace. Seal with sterilized jar lids, and process in a boiling water bath 15 minutes.

Makes 2 pints.

APPLE-JALAPEÑO SALSA

This is a good salsa to serve over fish or chicken.

2 medium Gala apples, cored and diced into ¼-inch pieces
2 tablespoons fresh lime juice

1 jalapeño pepper, finely chopped
½ cup chopped orange segments
½ cup finely chopped onion
½ cup finely chopped green pepper
2 cloves garlic, minced
2 tablespoons chopped fresh cilantro
1 tablespoon cider vinegar
½ teaspoon ground cumin
1 teaspoon corn oil

Toss diced apples immediately with lime juice in a glass bowl. Stir in remaining ingredients. Chill well before serving. Refrigerate leftovers.

Makes 3 cups.

NO-COOK CRANBERRY-APPLE-ORANGE RELISH

A tasty accompaniment to serve with turkey, pork or baked ham.

1 12-ounce bag cranberries, cleaned
2 Granny Smith apples, unpeeled, cored and cut into large chunks
⅓ cup sweet orange marmalade
⅓ cup granulated sugar
⅛ teaspoon ground cinnamon

Place all ingredients in a food processor. Using blade attachment, pulse until coarsely chopped. Spoon into a glass bowl; cover and chill in refrigerator at least 2 hours or up to 3 days. Refrigerate leftovers.

Makes about 3½ cups.

APPLE SYRUP

Top your pancakes with this good syrup.

2 cups unsweetened apple juice
¼ cup brown sugar, packed
2 tablespoons cornstarch
¼ teaspoon salt
¼ teaspoon ground nutmeg or ground cinnamon
1½ teaspoons lemon juice, optional

Mix all ingredients, except lemon juice, in a saucepan; bring to a boil, then reduce heat to medium. Cook and stir until thickened, about 4 minutes. Stir in lemon juice if desired. Refrigerate leftovers.

Makes 2 cups.

NELAN'S APPLE-FLAVORED SYRUP

Serve warm over apple waffles or pancakes.

1 cup maple flavored syrup
½ cup frozen apple juice concentrate, thawed
pinch ground cinnamon

Stir ingredients in a small saucepan over medium heat until mixture is warm. Pour syrup into a clean glass container. Refrigerate leftovers.

Makes 1½ cups.

Jams
Jellies
Preserves
Apple Butter

PEAR-APPLE JAM

Oh, to have an orchard with pears and apples!

2 cups peeled, cored and diced pears
2 cups peeled, cored and diced apples
1 lemon, grated rind and juice, discard seeds

Place all ingredients in a heavy nonreactive saucepan. Cook over low heat until sugar is dissolved, stirring often. Bring to a boil and cook rapidly until mixture is thick and clear. Immediately fill hot sterilized jars, leaving ½-inch headspace. Seal with sterilized jar lids, and process in a boiling water bath for 10 minutes.

Makes 1½ pints.

APPLE JELLY

Your family will love this homemade apple jelly.

**4 pounds tart apples, washed and quartered without peeling or
  removing core**
4 cups water
granulated sugar

Place apples and water in a nonreactive kettle; cover and cook over low heat until apples are tender. Pour mixture into a jelly bag and let drip.

For each cup of juice you get, use ¾ cup sugar. Cook only 3–4 cups of juice at a time. Pour juice into a heavy saucepan and bring to a rolling boil. Add sugar gradually; boil rapidly to a jelling stage, 220°–222°, or until two drops of jelly will run together off the side of a spoon. Skim any foam and immediately fill hot sterilized jars, leaving ½-inch headspace. Seal with sterilized jar lids and process in a boiling water bath for 5 minutes.

Makes about 1½ pints.

APPLE PRESERVES

Use apples with a little tart flavor for these preserves.

5 pounds brown sugar
1½ teaspoons grated fresh lemon rind
1 piece whole ginger root
3½ cups water
5 pounds apples, peeled, cored and cut into quarters

Mix sugar, lemon rind, ginger and water in a large, heavy nonreactive saucepan; bring mixture to a boil. Add apples; cook until tender. Remove apples from syrup and immediately pack them into hot sterilized jars. Heat syrup to boiling and immediately pour over apples to fill jars, leaving ½-inch headspace. Seal with sterilized jar lids and process in a boiling water bath for 20 minutes.

Makes about 5 pints.

APPLE BUTTER

Can you remember, as a child, spreading apple butter on plain white bread? Sister Helen always had plenty on hand!

5 pounds firm, medium, tart cooking apples
1½ quarts apple cider
3 cups granulated sugar
1 teaspoon ground cinnamon
1 teaspoon ground allspice
1 teaspoon ground cloves
¼ teaspoon ground nutmeg

Wash and slice apples without removing core, seeds or peel; place in a large nonreactive kettle. Add cider; boil 15 minutes or until apples are soft. Remove apples and press through a sieve (you should have about 3 quarts of pulp). Place pulp back into cider; gently boil 1 hour or until it begins to thicken, stirring often. Stir in sugar and spices. Cook over low heat 3 hours or until thickened, stirring often. Immediately fill hot sterilized jars, leaving ½-inch headspace. Seal with sterilized jar lids and process in a boiling water bath for 10 minutes.

Makes about 3¼ pints.

CROCK POT APPLE BUTTER

Homemade apple butter…a delicious spread for bread or biscuits!

16 cups ripe apples, washed, cored, unpeeled and chopped
2 cups apple cider
2 cups granulated sugar
2 teaspoons ground cinnamon
½ teaspoon ground cloves
pinch of ginger, nutmeg, mace and allspice

Mix apples and apple cider in crock pot. Cover and cook on low heat for 10–12 hours.

Remove from pot and puree in food mill, sieve or food processor. Return apple mixture to crock pot. Add sugar and spices. Cover and cook on low heat 6–10 hours. Pour hot mixture into hot sterilized jars. Seal and process in a boiling water bath for 10 minutes. May also be frozen in clean freezer containers for several months.

Makes 4 pints.

Miscellaneous

APLETS

Washington state is famous for this jellied-type fruit and nut candy.

2 tablespoons gelatin
1¼ cups applesauce, divided

2 cups granulated sugar
1 tablespoon cornstarch

1 tablespoon fresh lemon juice
1 teaspoon pure vanilla extract
⅔ cup chopped walnuts, toasted

powdered sugar

Soak gelatin and ½ cup applesauce in a bowl for 10 minutes; set aside.

Mix remaining ¾ cup applesauce, sugar and cornstarch in a medium saucepan. Bring to a boil, stirring constantly. Stir in gelatin-applesauce mixture until well blended; bring to a rolling boil, stirring constantly. Reduce heat to medium-high and continue boiling, stirring occasionally, 25 minutes. Remove from heat.

Stir in lemon juice, vanilla and chopped walnuts until well mixed. Pour into a greased 11x7-inch glass baking dish, or a greased 8x8-inch glass baking dish for a thicker candy. Let stand at room temperature 24–48 hours or until firm. When firm, cut into squares and roll in powdered sugar.

Makes about 3 dozen.

APPLE CHIPS

There is no need to core the apples, because boiling in juice for several minutes softens the core and removes the seeds.

2 cups unsweetened apple juice
1 cinnamon stick
2 Red Delicious apples

Bring apple juice and cinnamon stick to a slow boil in a large saucepan.

Slice off ½ inch from tops and bottoms of apples with a paring knife; discard. Stand apples on either cut end; cut crosswise into ⅛-inch-thick slices, rotating apple as necessary to cut even slices.

Drop slices into boiling juice; cook 4–5 minutes or until slices appear translucent and lightly golden.

Preheat oven to 250°.
Remove apple slices from juice with a slotted spoon; pat dry. Arrange slices on wire racks, making sure none overlap. Place racks on middle shelf in oven. Bake 30–40 minutes until slices are lightly browned and almost dry to touch. Let chips cool on racks completely before storing in airtight container.

Makes about 40 chips.

APPLE PEANUT BUTTER DIP

One delicious way to eat apples!

4 apples
1 cup orange juice

Dip
1 cup dairy sour cream or 1 8-ounce package cream cheese, softened
¾ cup brown sugar
1 teaspoon pure vanilla extract
½ cup crunchy peanut butter

Wash and core apples, but do not peel. Cut into ¼-inch slices. Place in a bowl and cover with orange juice; chill.

Mix all dip ingredients in a glass serving bowl. Drain apple slices and arrange on a platter. Serve with dip. Refrigerate leftovers.

Makes 8 servings.

APPLE-NUT GRANOLA

Apples, raisins, figs, apricots, almonds and pecans in this tasty granola.

3 cups oatmeal
⅔ cup sliced almonds
½ cup broken pecans
3 tablespoons hulled sunflower seeds
½ cup unsweetened coconut
½ teaspoon ground cinnamon
½ teaspoon salt

¼ cup butter
6 tablespoons honey
½ cup dried apple rings
¼ cup each: raisins, dried figs, dried apricots

Preheat oven to 325°.
Mix first seven ingredients in a large bowl.

Stir butter and honey in a small saucepan over low heat until butter melts.
Pour over mixture in large bowl; stir until combined.

Spread granola evenly in a large jelly-roll baking pan coated with cooking spray. Bake until golden brown, about 15 minutes, stirring after 8 minutes of baking. Place pan on a rack and cool completely.

Stir in dried fruit. Store at room temperature, in an airtight container, up to 2 weeks.

Makes about 7 cups.

CHOCOLATE PEANUT BUTTER FONDUE WITH APPLE DIPPERS

A warm tasty dip for fresh crisp apples.

⅓ **cup unsweetened cocoa powder**
⅓ **cup granulated sugar**
⅓ **cup milk**
3 tablespoons light corn syrup
2 tablespoons creamy peanut butter

½ teaspoon pure vanilla extract
3 medium apples, unpeeled, cored and sliced
12 large fresh strawberries

Mix first five ingredients in a medium saucepan. Cook over medium heat, stirring constantly, until hot. Remove from heat and stir in vanilla. Pour fondue into a medium serving bowl or fondue pot. Serve warm or at room temperature with apple and strawberry dippers. Refrigerate leftovers.

Makes 6 servings.

FAVORITE CARAMEL APPLES

Fresh tart apples dipped in homemade caramel.

10 tart apples, washed and dried
1 cup finely chopped salted peanuts

½ cup butter
2 cups brown sugar, packed
1 cup light corn syrup
pinch salt
1 14-ounce can sweetened condensed milk
1 teaspoon pure vanilla extract

Place a clean craft stick with rounded ends in stem end of each apple; set aside. Place peanuts in a small shallow bowl; set aside.

Melt butter in a 2-quart saucepan; add brown sugar, corn syrup and a pinch of salt. Cook over medium heat, stirring occasionally, until mixture comes to a full boil, about 10–12 minutes. Stir in sweetened condensed milk and continue cooking, stirring occasionally, until a small amount of mixture dropped into ice water forms a firm ball, or a candy thermometer reaches 245°, about 20–25 minutes. Remove from heat; stir in vanilla.

Dip apples into caramel, then dip top of each apple into peanuts. Place onto buttered waxed paper, stick side up. Serve or store in refrigerator.

Makes 10 servings.

TURTLE CARAMEL APPLES

A dream dessert on a stick!

1 cup coarsely chopped pecans, peanuts or macadamia nuts

6 Golden Delicious apples
1 14-ounce bag caramels, unwrapped
2 tablespoons water

½ cup semi-sweet chocolate chips
1 tablespoon solid shortening

Line a baking sheet with waxed paper; set aside.

Divide nuts equally into 6 piles on waxed paper; set aside.

Wash and dry apples completely. Insert a clean craft stick or popsicle stick into stem end of each apple.

Stir caramels and water in a small saucepan over very low heat until caramels are melted. Dip each apple into caramel, spooning caramel over apple to cover completely. Let excess drip back in saucepan. Immediately roll apples in nuts to lightly coat, pressing nuts lightly with fingers. Place apples stick-side up on prepared baking sheet.

Heat chocolate chips and shortening over low heat in a small saucepan, stirring until melted. Spoon chocolate over each apple and let it drizzle down sides. Let apples stand until chocolate is set, about 30 minutes. Serve or store loosely covered in refrigerator up to 3 days. Let stand at room temperature 15 minutes before serving.

Makes 6 servings.

Crab Apples

CRAB APPLE BUTTER

Crab apple butter...spreading-good on any bread.

4 pounds crab apples, unpeeled

For each cup of pulp, add:
½ cup granulated sugar
¾ teaspoon ground cloves
½ teaspoon allspice
2 teaspoons ground cinnamon

Wash and remove stems from apples. Cut into pieces. Place in a saucepot. Cover with 2 cups water. Cook until soft. Put cooked apples through a sieve or strainer.

Add the appropriate amounts of sugar and spices for the amount of pulp you get, following the list of ingredients.

Cook mixture in a saucepot over low heat, stirring constantly, until sugar is dissolved. Then increase heat and cook rapidly, stirring until it sheets from a spoon. Or to test, place a small amount on a saucer, and when no rim of liquid separates around the edge of the butter, it is done. Immediately pour into hot sterilized jars. Seal. Process in a boiling water bath for 10 minutes.

Makes about 5 pints.

CRAB APPLE JAM

Honey is used in this sweet jam.

5 quarts crab apples, unpeeled, washed
2 cups water

¼ cup fresh lemon juice
1 cup apple juice
½ cup water
1 package pectin
1⅓ cups honey

Put apples and 2 cups water in a large pot. Cook until apples start to pop, about 20 minutes. Press cooked apples through a sieve or food mill.

Place pulp into a large pot. Add lemon juice, apple juice and ½ cup water. Slowly add pectin, stirring until dissolved. Stir in honey. Bring to a full rolling boil; boil 1 minute. Remove from heat and immediately pour jam into hot sterilized jars. Seal with 2-piece canning lids. Process in a boiling water bath for 10 minutes.

Makes 8 half-pints.

CRAB APPLE JELLY

Good gift item...if you can part with it!

5 pounds crab apples
5 cups water

1 box fruit pectin, such as Sure Jell
9 cups granulated sugar, measured into separate bowl

Remove stems and blossom ends from unpeeled apples. Core apples and cut into small pieces. Place in a large saucepan; add water. Bring to a boil. Reduce heat to low; cover and simmer 10 minutes, stirring occasionally. Crush cooked apples; cover and simmer 5 minutes. Place 3 layers of damp cheesecloth or a jelly bag in a large bowl. Pour crushed apples into cheesecloth or bag; tie closed. Hang and let drip into bowl until dripping stops. Press gently. Measure exactly 7 cups of this juice into a 6-quart saucepot (add up to ½ cup water for exact measure).

Stir pectin into juice in saucepot. Bring to a full rolling boil over high heat, stirring constantly. Stir in sugar; return to full rolling boil and boil exactly 1 minute, stirring constantly. Remove from heat. Skim off any foam with a metal spoon.

Ladle jelly immediately into hot sterilized jars, leaving ⅛-inch headspace. Wipe jar rims and threads. Cover with 2-piece lids and screw bands on tightly. Process in a boiling water bath for 5 minutes. Cool; check seals by pressing middle of lid with finger. If lid springs back, lid is not sealed, and refrigeration is required.

Makes about 10 cups.

CRAB APPLE HOT PEPPER JELLY

Serve as a condiment for pork or chicken. Also good with cream cheese.

2 pounds crab apples
1½ cups water
red wine vinegar
3¾ cups granulated sugar
1 cup green bell pepper
⅓ cup hot peppers

Wash apples. Place in a large pot with water. Cover and bring to a simmer. Cook until crab apples are very soft. Pour into a colander that has been lined with a square of dampened cheesecloth and placed over a deep bowl. Place a saucer over cheesecloth mixture, and place a heavy weight over saucer. Let stand until dripping stops. Discard pulp.

In a sauce pan, pour juice and enough red wine vinegar to measure 3 cups. Stir in sugar. Bring to a rolling boil, stirring constantly. Add peppers, and boil briskly 8–10 minutes or until set. To test for set, remove pan from heat. Dip a cold metal spoon into the liquid and hold it well above the steam. Turn spoon sideways and let liquid run off. When it forms two drops that run together and drip from edge, jelling point has been reached. Stir for 7 minutes to prevent floating peppers.

Immediately pour jelly into hot sterilized canning jars. Seal with two-piece canning lids. Process in a boiling water bath for 5 minutes.

Makes 6 half-pints.

CRAB APPLE QUICK BREAD

Serve with softened cream cheese or butter.

2 eggs
1 cup granulated sugar
½ cup shortening
2 tablespoons buttermilk
1 teaspoon pure vanilla extract
2 cups chopped, unpeeled crab apples

2 cups all-purpose flour
1 teaspoon baking soda
½ teaspoon salt
½ teaspoon ground cinnamon
¼ teaspoon ground nutmeg
⅛ teaspoon ground cloves

½ cup chopped walnuts

Preheat oven to 350°.
Beat eggs in a bowl. Add sugar and shortening; beat until creamy. Stir in buttermilk, vanilla and apples.

Mix flour, soda, salt and spices in another bowl; stir into creamed mixture. Stir in chopped nuts. Pour into a greased and floured 9x5-inch loaf pan. Bake about 1 hour or until a wooden pick inserted in center comes out clean. Cool in pan 10 minutes, then remove from pan and cool on a wire rack. Refrigerate leftovers.

Makes 1 loaf.

GREEN APPLE-CRAB APPLE PIE

Share a slice with your neighbor!

pastry for a 9-inch double pie crust

Filling
½ cup granulated sugar
¼ cup brown sugar, packed
¼ cup all-purpose flour
½ teaspoon ground cinnamon
½ teaspoon ground nutmeg
5 cups peeled Granny Smith apples, sliced ¼-inch thick
1 cup sliced unpeeled crab apples
1 tablespoon butter, melted
1 teaspoon granulated sugar

Preheat oven to 400°.
Place 1 unbaked pie crust into a 9-inch pie pan; pressing firmly against bottom and sides. Trim crust to ½ inch from edge of pan; set aside.

Mix all filling ingredients except butter, 1 teaspoon sugar and apples in a large bowl. Add apples; toss until coated. Spoon into prepared crust. Place remaining unbaked crust over filling. Trim, seal and crimp or flute edge. Cut 5 large slits in crust. Brush with melted butter and sprinkle with 1 teaspoon sugar. Cover edge of crust with a 2-inch strip aluminum cooking foil.

Bake 35 minutes. Remove foil, and continue baking 10–20 minutes or until crust is lightly browned and juice begins to bubble through slits. Let stand 30 minutes before serving. Refrigerate leftovers.

Makes 8 servings.

SPICED CRAB APPLES

One good way to use all those crab apples.

5 pounds crab apples
4½ cups apple vinegar (5% acidity)
4 cups water
7½ cups granulated sugar

4 teaspoons whole cloves
4 cinnamon sticks
6 ½-inch cubes fresh ginger root

Wash apples and remove blossom petals, but leave stems attached. Make four puncture holes with a sharp pick in the skin of each apple.

Stir vinegar, water and sugar a heavy saucepot; bring to a boil. Tie spices in a spice bag and add to vinegar mixture.

Place one-third of the apples in boiling vinegar mixture; cook 2 minutes. Repeat with remaining apples. Place apples and spice bag in a 1-gallon crock; add vinegar mixture. Cover and let stand 8 hours. Remove spice bag. Drain vinegar mixture into a saucepan; bring to a boil.

Fill sterilized pint jars with apples and hot vinegar mixture, leaving ½-inch headspace. Adjust lids and process in a boiling water bath for 20 minutes.

Makes about 9 pints.

About the Author

Theresa Millang is a popular and versatile cookbook author. She has written successful cookbooks on muffins, brownies, pies, cookies, cheesecake, casseroles and several on Cajun cooking. She has cooked on television, and contributed many recipes to food articles throughout the U.S.A.

Theresa's other cookbooks
I Love Cheesecake
I Love Pies You Don't Bake
The Muffins Are Coming

Theresa's other current cookbooks
The Best of Cajun-Creole Recipes
The Best of Chili Recipes
The Great Minnesota Hot Dish
The Joy of Blueberries
The Joy of Rhubarb
The Joy of Cranberries

Notes